More Praise for

INTERCONNECTED

"This important book will convince you that a commitment to social and environmental justice flows naturally from mindfulness of interdependence. The Karmapa's vision of a heart-centered spiritual practice fills one with hope, even as it addresses the most serious challenges facing us today. One of the most influential Tibetan Buddhist teachers of our times, the Karmapa has written a courageous book that will change how you see your place in the world—and inspire you to act to make it a happier and kinder one."

—SHARON SALZBERG, author of *Lovingkindness*

"The book records with unassuming clarity the Karmapa's meditations on interbeing—individual and collective. Any reader who approaches it with an open heart will be richly rewarded."

—JOHN STANLEY, director of Ecological Buddhism

"During this time of what our people know as the crossroads, it is an honor to walk through this time with a Peace Keeper who understands the significance of sacred sites and that Mother Earth is the source of life, not a resource. In a circle of life where there is no ending and no beginning, *Onipikte*—We shall live."

—NAC'A (CHIEF) ARVOL LOOKING HORSE, Lakota, Dakota, and Nakota Nations

"Highly intelligent and filled with honesty, personal reflection, and striking insights on every page, this book urges us not only to understand our interdependence intellectually but also to cultivate an embodied awareness of it, both for our own evolution and as a path to living our lives as helpful and responsible world citizens."

—JANET GYATSO, Hershey Professor of Buddhist Studies, Harvard Divinity School

"Now more than ever, His Holiness the Karmapa's teachings provide tools for all of us—beyond background, nationality, and culture—to work together in our interdependent, interconnected worldwide community. Everyone, and the world itself, will benefit from the profound teachings in this book."

—PEMA CHÖDRÖN, author of *When Things Fall Apart*

"Marvelous. *Interconnected* provides the Buddha's prescription of care, responsibility, and engaged practice. Anyone who loves the world will benefit and be nourished by this book."

—KOSHIN PALEY ELLISON, editor of *Awake at the Bedside*

"For two hundred years the dominant paradigm of reductionism and fragmentation has created the illusion that we are separate from nature. We have violated the very processes that maintain life. His Holiness the Karmapa invites us to be aware of our connections with the natural and social worlds that are the condition of our being as he gently walks us through a journey to courageous compassion. This book should be read by everyone—young and old, Buddhist and non-Buddhist. It is a survival guide for humanity."

—DR. VANDANA SHIVA, environmental activist and author of *Earth Democracy: Justice, Sustainability, and Peace*

INTERCONNECTED

Embracing Life in Our Global Society

The Karmapa,
Ogyen Trinley Dorje

*Edited by Karen Derris
and Damchö Diana Finnegan*

Wisdom Publications
199 Elm Street
Somerville, MA 02144 USA
wisdompubs.org

The Library of Congress has cataloged the hardcover edition as follows:
Names: O-rgyan-'phrin-las-rdo-rje, Karma-pa XVII, 1985– author. |
    Derris, Karen, editor. | Finnegan, Damchö Diana, editor.
Title: Interconnected: embracing life in our global society / Karmapa Ogyen Trinley
    Dorje; edited by Karen Derris and Damchö Diana Finnegan.
Description: Somerville, MA: Wisdom Publications, 2017.
Identifiers: LCCN 2016033500 (print) | LCCN 2016048202 (ebook) |
    ISBN 9781614294122 (hardcover: alk. paper) | ISBN 1614294127 (hardcover: alk.
    paper) | ISBN 9781614294207 () | ISBN 1614294208 ()
Subjects: LCSH: Buddhism. | Conduct of life. | Globalization—Religious aspects—
    Buddhism.
Classification: LCC BQ4012 .O74 2017 (print) | LCC BQ4012 (ebook) | DDC
    294.3/444—dc23
LC record available at https://lccn.loc.gov/2016033500

ISBN 978-1-61429-521-1   ebook ISBN 978-1-61429-420-7

21 20 19 18
4 3 2 1

Cover design by Phil Pascuzzo. Interior design by Gopa&Ted2, Inc.
Set in Sabon LT Pro 10.4/15.8. Author photo by Gao Yuaner.

Wisdom Publications' books are printed on acid-free paper and meet
the guidelines for permanence and durability of the Production Guidelines
for Book Longevity of the Council on Library Resources.

♻ This book was produced with environmental mindfulness.
For more information, please visit wisdompubs.org/wisdom-environment.

Printed in the United States of America.

Please visit fscus.org

Contents

Editors' Introduction

W HAT WOULD IT TAKE for people to stop treating happiness as a zero-sum game and start living with confidence that mutual flourishing was not only possible but realistic? To pose such a question may strike some readers as either naive or daunting, but given the challenges facing our world today, this is the kind of shift we need to explore with an open mind and a sincere willingness to act within the possible. In this book, His Holiness the Karmapa shows how much we could change in the world by approaching our lives as profoundly interconnected rather than seeing ourselves as discrete and ultimately separate individuals.

Over the course of the book, the Karmapa offers a sustained reflection on what it would mean to undertake such a paradigm shift particularly in the context of our electronic connectivity. To begin with, he argues, communications technologies are already making our interconnectedness more apparent to us. Acknowledgment of this radically different paradigm is already gaining traction in popular perception, in activist circles, and in intellectual discourse. From a world of siloed societies and independent individuals, many people have begun to recognize that we are interconnected communities and interdependent individuals. Thinkers and activists in fields as far flung as economics, earth sciences, and social justice are collectively creating a multidisciplinary account of the diverse ways that our world functions interdependently. Empirical research provides ample evidence indicating that interconnections operate in every social and natural arena. While the use of the paradigm of interdependence is still relatively new in scientific, academic, activist, and other discussions, the idea that all phenomena are interconnected has formed the basis of Buddhist thought and ethics since its outset.

This book aims to add the voice of His Holiness the Karmapa to present-day conversations that explore global issues through the lens of interdependence. He joins important discussions already urging greater awareness of the instances and effects of interdependence in the world. The Karmapa is particularly concerned with ensuring that our heightened awareness leads to changes in individual and collective behavior, to help build a global society that works in concert with rather than resistant to the realities of interdependence. At the age of thirty-one, he is already a major thinker deeply engaged in environmental and social justice issues, as well as the head of a 900-year-old Tibetan Buddhist lineage and one of Buddhism's most important spiritual leaders. Although the Karmapa is steeped in Buddhist philosophical traditions in which interdependence is a central tenet, he makes very little use of Buddhist terminology to discuss interconnection and claims no particular authority for himself in speaking on these issues. His concern in this book is not primarily to define a Buddhist position on interdependence for those exploring it as a theory, but in exploring the possibilities for social and ethical transformation that interdependence opens up. As a result, this is neither a book about Buddhism nor a particularly Buddhist book. Rather, it is an open process of thinking collaboratively on the basis of our shared human condition and shared concerns for the world.

One unique contribution the Karmapa makes is in extending the discussion to include the working of interconnectedness within us—

what he calls *inner interdependence*. The discourse thus far has tended to focus primarily on the principle of interdependence at work in our external conditions—in the natural world and in social and economic phenomena. The Karmapa demonstrates that our inner domain is also a site where interdependence takes place, and he makes a strong case that an analysis of conditions that combine to shape our world interdependently must also include our inner conditions if it is to lead to social and environmental change.

As empirical investigation has made clear, our external reality is shaped through the interplay of myriad conditions. Among those conditions, some of the most influential are human attitudes and actions. Our perceptions, ideas, interpretations, and emotions interact, shaping how we experience our connections, how we respond, and what we contribute to those connections. As such, our inner conditions have a real impact on the external world, and therefore investigation of the dynamics of interdependence at work in the world around us is incomplete without a consideration of the world within us.

The role of emotional awareness is a second major theme running through the book. For the Karmapa, emotions serve as a force that is essential for translating intellectual understanding into positive action. The Karmapa argues that it is not sufficient to *know* we are interconnected. We must learn to *feel* connected, as the necessary basis for acting in ways that reflect our interconnectedness. Gathering and analyzing data that demonstrates our interdependence has been an important first step. Cultivating emotional experience and awareness of interconnection is the crucial next step if we are to transform patterns of individual and collective action so that they are coherent with interdependence. Empathy has already received attention in other works as an important ethical quality for an interdependent world; here the Karmapa greatly expands the category to include such virtues as courage, contentment, patience, responsibility, mental agility, and imagination. In his presentation, just as empathy gains meaning when it moves us to compassionate action, so too does responsibility when it is embraced as opportunity. As such, human virtues are radically reoriented as values for living and acting wisely in an interconnected world.

The title of this book—*Interconnected: Embracing Life in Our Global Society*—makes use of the term "interconnected," rather than "interdependent," precisely to draw attention to the human, affective dimension of our interdependence, in contrast to the external phenomena more often referenced by the term "interdependence." The Karmapa uses "interdependence" and "interconnectedness" almost interchangeably, and the Tibetan term itself (*rten cing 'brel bar 'byung ba*) is a compound that includes the terms that denote dependence and connection. The book is divided in three sections, corresponding to the three phases that move us from intellectual to emotional awareness and from there to action—understanding that we are interconnected, feeling our connectedness, and acting in ways consistent with it.

An ethics of interdependence emerges through these three sections of the book. The Karmapa proceeds by first laying an ontological foundation—that is, by describing the interdependent nature of who we are and the world we live in—and goes on to identify innate emotional qualities and ethical virtues we can cultivate that are suited to such a foundation. Some of the inner qualities and social values explored in this book—such as empathy, contentment, and freedom—shape how we experience our connections to others, while others—such as responsibility, courage, and compassion—mobilize our ethical actions in relation to them. In this way, the Karmapa's vision of an ethics of interdependence moves well beyond descriptive theory, offering a generative model for social and ethical change.

Although the fact that there is a link between understanding and behavioral change hardly requires stating, it is clear that the advances in our intellectual recognition of interconnection have not created sufficient conditions for motivating effective action, as countless examples demonstrate. The availability of data detailing the connections between world hunger and the high level of environmental resources required to feed cattle has yet to change our dietary practices; investigative reporting on substandard working conditions of factory workers in the Global South producing goods for luxury markets in the North has yet to lead to widespread or significant changes in consumption or corporate labor practices. Intellectual understanding is necessary but not sufficient for sustainable connection of awareness to effective action. In this book, the Karmapa points to emotional engagement as the element that must be cultivated in order to transform patterns of individual and collective actions so that they are coherent with interdependence.

The discussion in this book builds upon work begun in his earlier book, *The Heart Is Noble: Changing the World from the Inside Out*, in which the Karmapa explored a series of personal, social, and environmental issues where individuals can contribute to creating a sustainable, compassionate world. In *Interconnected: Embracing Life in Our Global Society*, he offers us a focused and sustained exploration of interdependence itself. The aim of his argument is to illuminate its ethical and social implications for global society in this age of connectivity. The Karmapa's pragmatic approach keeps us oriented toward the goal of positive change and keeps visible the basic questions: What are the conditions necessary for happiness? How can we create them, individually and collectively? What are the conditions that cause suffering? How can we end them?

The Karmapa is a vocal critic of the global conditions human beings have created that have led to human, animal, and environmental harm. His sustained critique of global consumerist culture alerts us to our vulnerability to manipulation when we do not live our interdependence wisely. He similarly cautions that we must be much more conscious in our use of technology, as too often our current modes of engaging online leave us more disconnected than ever. Yet the Karmapa also sees great potential in technology as a means to connect to others, as he himself does through his frequent webcasts of his teachings, and suggests methods to avoid reproducing harmful ways of relating to others online.

In *Interconnected*, the Karmapa makes clear just how radically different the model of interdependence is from dominant models of discrete individuals, communities, and things. Taken to its logical conclusion, the fact that we are thoroughly interconnected means that self and other are not ultimately separable on individual or societal levels. This fundamental insight has far-reaching ramifications for all our relationships—to other beings, to things, to the planet, and to our own ideas and experiences. It can profoundly reshape the emotional and social landscape in which we live out our lives and thoroughly reorient us within that landscape. In the process, we are challenged to rethink who we are as individuals and how we engage with and are shaped by the world. The goal throughout is to open up new possibilities for living interdependently with and for others.

The way in which this book came about is an example of the vision of living interdependence that His Holiness presents within it. The book's content originated in a series of teachings His Holiness offered to a group of undergraduate students from the University of Redlands, a liberal-arts university in California. The students had traveled to Dharamsala, India, with Professor Karen Derris for three weeks of study with the Karmapa facilitated by Venerable Damchö Diana Finnegan. The Karmapa met with the students in his library for sessions that began with student presentations of their concerns and questions, to which His Holiness responded with extensive reflections. Under the guidance of the Karmapa, Damchö and Karen subsequently edited these teachings into the present book. This was the second time the Karmapa had received a class from the University of Redlands in his residence, and *Interconnected* is the second book such exchanges have yielded.

That His Holiness chooses to articulate his thoughts through exchanging views with others of diverse culture, religion, and life experience—rather than penning his thoughts alone in his study as so many thinkers do—demonstrates his profound commitment to processes that reflect our basic interconnectedness. Through this process, the Karmapa showed himself to be a remarkably responsive thinker, even as his responses often challenged us to rethink the very premises of the students' questions. As the Karmapa addressed them, he suggested possibilities for other beginning points, created space for reflection upon previously unexamined assumptions, and built into other questions.

As a thinker, His Holiness is both challenging and dynamic, capable of holding multiple perspectives without the expectation that his conversation partners will approach the topic from any single orientation. Even as he invited us to view our lives through new vantage points that his teachings opened up, he displayed a consistent willingness to consider other people's vantage points as well. The Karmapa's mode of engaging with us provided the example of what he was describing—allowing others to form part of one's own self while committing to forming a condition for others' flourishing.

In 2013, when the teachings in this book were first given, His Holiness frequently reflected on the events of the day—including the collapse of a textile factory in Bangladesh and the Boston Marathon bombing. In the intervening years, the escalating number of terrorist attacks and the ongoing plight of refugees worldwide have offered further visceral proof that our response to our interconnectedness can produce either human suffering or flourishing. As this book is being finalized, voters in any number of nations are being asked to choose between working with interdependence on the one hand, or pulling up drawbridges and withdrawing behind walls. By the time readers are taking up this book, surely many more examples will have mounted to indicate that we are living in a historical period in which choices are being made between divergent models for relating to each other, with some people greatly inspired by the possibilities that interdependence offers and others resistant to the changes in behavior and lifestyle it would entail.

As the reader will see, the Karmapa frequently shared not only current events but also his own experiences and feelings. Indeed, he drew on his own life to provide the empirical material for reflection upon interdependence as part of our embodied, direct experience. As such, he was modeling a way that readers can explore the ideas he proposes by applying them as a means of reflection upon our own life experiences.

Although the Karmapa often draws on experience as a resource from which to elicit theories, experience is not merely a means to reach a theoretical end. Instead, theoretical positions are offered and shifted as part of a dynamic process in which the aim is to find the angle of vision that is most productive for cultivating emotional awareness and effective action. As His Holiness encourages us to shift lenses, he is offering a model for reading his book. We are invited to adopt various perspectives in examining our own experiences and relating to the world around us. As the Karmapa both describes and displays in this book, personal cultivation is a process that we engage in by trying out different options. This book offers readers the opportunity to bring their own experiences and contexts into their encounter with the vision the Karmapa outlines, and to bring them into conversation with the reflections in this book.

Because the interactions with the students in Dharamsala in 2013 were intended from the outset to be published as a book, the presence of its readers was continually anticipated and imagined in the process. The conversations were understood to be initiating an ongoing process in which the readers of this book would be active participants, through questioning assumptions, examining experiences, and rethinking ways of being and acting.

The Karmapa is, above all, interested in bringing about positive collective change in the world and understands that that requires collective action. He is optimistic about the basic human capacity for goodness, and about the possibilities that open up when we begin to embrace our interconnectedness. At the same time, he is highly realistic about the adverse conditions already in effect, and about the amount of work that is yet to be accomplished before we respond fully to the needs of a world that is crying out for social and environmental justice. Given the challenges ahead, and all that is at stake, there is a great need for voices like that of the Karmapa to guide us in cultivating the inner conditions to do so.

As he offers his own reflections as a condition for such change, he welcomes us to join him in the open, ongoing process of effecting positive change for our global society. This book itself is our open invitation to do so.

SEEING THE CONNECTION

ONE

Our Interdependent World

OUR WORLD IN THE twenty-first century is smaller than it used to be. People from widely dispersed societies are in closer contact than ever before, and just as importantly, we are more aware of our closeness. In this age of information, experts and ordinary observers alike can identify many ways that actions in one part of the world have far-reaching effects elsewhere on the planet. Awareness is growing that we live in a world where all of us, and the natural world that sustains us, are profoundly and radically connected.

This interconnection has long been described in Buddhism as *interdependence*, and that term now forms part of conversations far beyond Buddhist contexts. Professionals in diverse fields increasingly find interdependence to be an important framework for explaining what they observe. Environmental scientists find it indispensable for understanding ecosystems, economists apply it to international trade, and social theorists use it to chart the systems that reproduce racial and gender injustice, just to name a few.

Interdependence may be used to explain a great many systems, from the relationships among natural phenomena to groups of people and nations—in other words, the world around us. But I believe that an understanding of our deep interconnection can do far more than that. Interdependence is not a mere theory or interesting philosophy. It impacts our lives directly every single day. By deepening our awareness of interconnectedness, we can create a far more harmonious and healthy society and live far more satisfying lives. For that to happen, we can't just stop our analysis at the interdependence of the physical world. The human heart and mind—what we might call our inner world—form an integral part of these webs of interdependence.

Inside each of us is a complex constellation of perceptions, ideas, feelings, and intentions that mutually affect one another. Our inner worlds interact with outer conditions to shape the world around us. We respond to external circumstances, but we also create them. In other words, our inner worlds and the outer world are intimately connected, and that interconnection is part of interdependence as well. Recognizing the full extent of interdependence will lead to a fundamental rethinking of who we are as human beings and of our place in the world we help create.

Our inner world is the pivotal domain for bringing about real change in the world that we all share. Neither social nor environmental justice is possible without significant changes in our attitudes and the intentional behavior they give rise to. The transformation of our social and material world must begin within us.

The intellectual awareness we are gaining about interdependence is an important first step. The next—and crucial—step is to gain an emotional awareness of interdependence. We need to *feel* our profound interconnectedness and not just know about it. We have within us numerous qualities that help sustain such an emotional engagement with our interdependence. By enhancing our understanding of the interdependence of our inner world, we become better able to cultivate such qualities.

Once we do, the emotional awareness we have gained will profoundly reorient our relationships to others and our ways of being in the world. We will begin acting in ways that truly reflect our interdependence. When our understanding of interdependence has moved from head to heart and into action, our lives become fully effective and meaningful.

WHY (AND HOW) INTERDEPENDENCE MATTERS

Our interconnectedness matters in all our relationships and in every aspect of our lives. Interdependence is a definite force in the world. It has great value for us. Because of it, we can respond and adapt to circumstances. We can change. We can work toward our goals by gathering the conditions needed to accomplish them. If we were not interdependent, we would be unable to do any of that. Understanding how this fundamental principle works in our lives enables us to consciously reorient our lives and to change the world itself.

Interdependence describes our deep connectedness, but it also explains why and how we are interconnected. We can start by observing that everything in life happens due to various causes and conditions coming together. Interdependence reveals the profound implications of this simple fact. It shows us that everything that exists is a condition that affects others, and is affected in turn, in a vast and complex web of causality. As part of that web, we ourselves are a condition that impacts those around us. That means if we change, so do others.

As we can see, not only is the physical realm intimately interconnected; social systems are also subject to interdependence. So is our emotional life; so is everything, material or immaterial. Once we begin to look for it, we find interdependence no matter where we direct our gaze: from the largest astronomical systems to subtle shifts in our sensations. Interdependence has practical consequences in virtually every sphere of life on this planet. In fact, it has environmental, economic, social, psychological, and ethical implications that we as a global society have only just begun to fathom.

In the broadest view, the health of our planet depends on our recognizing how interdependence works in the natural world and especially how human actions—greatly amplified by technological advances—are interacting with other forces. On a personal level, our ability to find lasting happiness also depends on understanding how interdependence works within our own life and relationships. In short, the well-being of our global society as well as our individual happiness both depend on our learning how to live fully in tune with our interdependence.

To recognize the workings of interdependence in our inner as well as in the outer world, we must ask some basic questions. How would the way we relate to others change if we began to *feel* our interconnectedness? What human values come to the fore when we acknowledge our interdependence emotionally as well as intellectually? What would a global society that fully embraced interdependence look like? What can we ourselves do to help create that society?

WHAT IS TRULY YOURS?

In Buddhism, applying the view of interdependence leads us to examine the nature of the self, and it challenges how we see ourselves in relation to others. That rethinking transforms how we engage with others, emotionally and in our actions.

We can start by observing our own experience. From the vantage point of interdependence, we can begin to see that our connections to others cannot be severed. Our happiness and suffering are so closely connected to the happiness and suffering of others as to be inseparable. This means that no individual is fully self-sustaining or divisible from others.

To see whether this rings true, reflect on what you are referring to when you say "I" or "me." Most likely you will find that you are thinking of yourself as solid and separate, as a truly independent entity. But is there such a thing? When you say "I," if asked to specify what exactly you are referring to, you will invariably point to your own body. Where else would you point? But this body came from others. Your body developed from cellular material provided by your two biological parents. Without them, it would not have come to exist.

After those cells began dividing, your body formed and grew based on all the nutrients you received. The physical form you have today is the product of what you first received in the womb, followed by a whole lifetime of meals. Those meals were mostly prepared by other people and made of ingredients that come entirely from resources outside of yourself, namely plants and animals. Since there is no such thing as a living body that did not grow based on what it takes in from its environment, nor any human being that did not come from parents, your body is not in reality a separate *you*. It comes from others. Your body exists because of many factors that you think of as other than you. Therefore it is not entirely correct to call it *me*. But neither is it someone other than you.

In my own case, my father is named Karma Dondrup and my mother is Lolaga. My features bear some resemblance to theirs, as my body originates from the combination of their DNA. Basically, I was produced by them, much as a product is produced by a company. You could even say I bear their mark. Unlike an industrial product produced in a factory, our parents do not literally stamp a label or a brand on our body, even if parents do act sometimes as if they held the copyright to their children!

If you cannot point to your body as *me*, what about the other things you think of as *mine*? There is the clothing you wear. It was made by others and acquired from others. Before it was *yours*, you either had to purchase it from somewhere, or someone had to give it to you as a gift. None of us was born wearing clothing. Cotton comes from plants, wool comes from the body of sheep who had to be forcibly parted from it in order for it to become yours, and synthetic fabrics are produced in factories. Many other human beings and even some animals have a hand in the clothes you now think of as *yours*. Every time you put on clothes, or enjoy a cup of tea or a plate of food, you are witnessing this display of your interdependence, for these are all prepared and served to you by others, directly or indirectly.

All of these things that we think of as *me* and *mine*—our bodies, our clothes, our food, and all our material possessions—come from others. So where is this *I* that is exclusively me? We seem to be left with nothing that is uniquely our own. Yet we still continue to say "I" when it should be evident that 99 percent of what we call *I* is not really I. It is what we usually consider "other."

The 1 percent you might quibble about is your consciousness. Yet you would have a very hard time arguing that your thoughts are wholly unconnected to others, unless all your thoughts are absolutely original and you think in a language that is unique to you. Not only our ideas, but a great deal of our emotional life and our psychological makeup is very clearly influenced by others and impacted by what goes on around us.

Even were it the case that our basic awareness or consciousness were truly and exclusively ours while perhaps the other 99 percent is not, it is not that 1 percent that we are thinking of primarily when we say "I." When we say "I," we mean the entire complex of body and mind. We are referring to the whole package, as it were, and we have seen that 99 percent of that package is what we normally consider to be other—coming from plants and animals, and deeply marked by the presence of many other human beings. After thinking about it in this way—from the viewpoint of interdependence—ask yourself whether there is such a thing as an entirely independent you.

What you think of and hold onto as yourself is actually a product of others; many causes and conditions contributed to the creation of who you are. But it is not sufficient to simply acknowledge this. Understanding the fact of your interdependence intellectually will not transform your experience. But reflecting in this way deeply is a starting point for cultivating the feelings of our connections to others.

The aim is to be able to feel the extent to which others are extremely important and integral to you and also to gain an emotional awareness that you are never, ever really separate from them. Others are part of you, just as you are part of them. You exist in connection with others. When you see this, you can also see that your happiness and suffering depend upon others. If you think solely in terms of yourself and your own happiness, it simply does not work. There is no happiness without relying upon others.

Once we deeply understand that self and others are not two entirely distinct things—that we are not really separate—many things can change. We will feel a sense of profound connection to other beings, and we will experience their contributions to who we are with gratitude and goodwill. We will see and feel that we simply must consider others' well-being.

THE WONDER OF BREATHING

We can also extend these feelings of intimate connectedness to our natural environment. Turning our attention to the most basic condition for our life on this planet—the air we breathe—we see that we cannot be separated from our physical environment. Even if we could manage for some time without food or clothing, we cannot survive more than a few minutes without oxygen. A vast number of conditions need to come together to yield the uninterrupted supply of oxygen that is indispensable to keep us alive, yet we ourselves make no conscious effort to bring those conditions about. Contemplating this basic fact can spark a sense of wonder and gratitude toward the planet itself.

What's more, we ourselves form part of this vast system of

symbiotic exchanges. As the trees and plants take in sunlight and carbon dioxide to produce the oxygen that we so vitally require, we are continually reciprocating with carbon dioxide, which plants use as they produce more oxygen. Once we inhale, that oxygen is carried by our blood to cells throughout our body. Thus we can say that trees and plants and the sun itself are present in our every cell, just as our breath may be present in the plants' cells.

Viewing our place in the world in this way, we see more fully that everything required for us to come into being, all that we turn to in order to define who we are, and everything we need to survive in life is connected to other people and to resources outside of ourselves. Likewise, we are resources that others depend upon for their existence. Who and what we are is inextricably and reciprocally linked to others.

Maintaining this awareness as we live our lives can help us move beyond a merely intellectual understanding of interdependence. As we increasingly apply this lens to our experiences, the awareness moves from our head to our heart, and we can begin to actually experience ourselves as interconnected. Our observations become the basis for new understanding and new feelings. This in turn can spark a fundamental reorientation toward others and our place in an interdependent world.

NOURISHING THE WORLD

Buddhist texts use an analogy to describe the relationship between us living beings and the natural environment. This analogy can also help us see a deeper implication of interdependence. The natural world is described as a container, and all the beings that live in it are described as its contents. This analogy emphasizes the inextricable connection of humans, animals, and their natural environment. The planet holds and sustains us. Without it, we would literally fall apart.

When we think of containers, we often overlook the ways in which the contents can affect the container itself—warming or cooling it, staining or bleaching it, stretching or strengthening it and even breaking it. The word used in Tibetan for "contents" in this analogy also literally means "nutrients," such that we ourselves are like the nourishment for the world that contains us. Indeed, as I have mentioned, the carbon dioxide we exhale nourishes the trees and plants, and our bodies also return to the earth and nourish it after we have died. The natural environment, in turn, nourishes us and provides us with the conditions we need for life. What this signals is that the connections of interdependence between us and the world we live in are far closer and more reciprocal than we normally envision.

This analogy can render the fact of interdependence very vivid for us—to help take it beyond a mere idea and make it something we can actually feel, live, and breathe. This is important, because interdependence is not a theoretical possibility—it's a practical reality.

ALL RELATIONSHIPS GO BOTH WAYS

Human beings' relationship of dependence with the planet does not go in only one direction, though for most of history we seem to have overlooked that fact. When we think of earthquakes, blizzards, or floods, we readily recognize that natural phenomena have an impact on us. What is less obvious is that we too impact the planet and that our actions can either harm or benefit it.

Not only are we are affecting the world; we appear to be in the process of making it uninhabitable. Some may find it difficult to see how we could nurture the earth, but the fact that we are damaging it has become hard to deny. When contents are corrosive, they damage the container. If we keep in mind the analogy of container and contents, it might help us see that interdependence always works both ways. Although many people now do acknowledge this, that admission has not yet led to the next crucial step—sufficient changes in our behavior to stop the harm and create the conditions for the earth to start healing.

Of course, we are not entirely blind to the fact of our basic interconnectedness to the planet. It is more a matter of having too limited a range of view. The earth is so immense, it is hard to see the impact we have. But our individual acts participate in far-reaching processes of causality all the time. We just need to cultivate different lenses so we can gain awareness of our interdependence on both vast and intimate scales.

All parties are changed by being in relationship. Just being connected to someone or something means we are each forming part of the other. This is true in all forms of interdependence, from those that form planetary systems to our most intimate and personal relationships. For example, in the case of parents and children, although in the more obvious sense parents produce children, yet it is only by having children that people become parents. We could even say that parents are born in the moment that their first child comes into their life. Before they had children, a woman and man were not a mother or father. In that sense, children also make their parents *parents*. Interdependence connects us on many levels and always works both ways.

NATURE IS NOT SCENERY

Recognizing our intimate dependence on the natural environment allows us to see its true value and treasure it. One reason that people living in cities nowadays need to be told so much about the importance of caring for the earth is because they did not grow up feeling direct, unmediated connections to it. For them, nature is something that one visits in city parks or on excursions out into the countryside. When we are raised in urban environments, our sense for the natural environment is more remote because we rarely witness our fundamental reliance upon it. Nature seems like a pretty backdrop to our lives, something that adds to the scenery but is basically optional. We are obstructed from seeing how the natural environment is the very stage on which our lives play out. Without the conditions that arise from our environment, nothing whatsoever can take place.

In my own case, I was born and spent the early part of my life in a pristine environment in the highlands of the Tibetan plateau. My family were nomads, and we adjusted our lives to the rhythm of the seasons. We lived in tents, in constant direct touch with the earth. When I first left my homeland, I remember that for a long time I experienced a physical longing to return and reconnect, to plant my feet on that earth once again and inhale the freshness of the high-altitude breezes. Moreover, the sky in eastern Tibet is wide open and the land is spacious. Nowadays when I'm in an urban setting with streets like narrow canyons, it can feel a bit like the buildings are closing in on me. Added to that, the experience of the city's cement sidewalks is far removed from that of touching the living earth.

Of course even if we aren't born in rural environments, we can cultivate a closer appreciation for the natural world. We can seek out opportunities to come into direct sensory contact with nature, smelling the soil, listening to running water, or touching the bark of a tree. There is much to be said for sensory experiences as a way to feel our personal interconnectedness in a vivid and unmediated way. As our senses open, our heart is moved. This direct experience evokes affection and closeness, and that leads naturally to wanting to nurture and protect our planet.

I have been inspired to dedicate effort to environmental issues, and I definitely credit this to my childhood immersion in nature. My involvement with environmental preservation also mitigates my sense of distance from the natural environment in which I was born. This experience makes me believe that we can alleviate our alienation from nature by becoming courageous in our efforts to care for the environment as a whole.

RIPPLE EFFECTS

Interdependence involves causality—the way things happen due to the coming together of certain causes and conditions. The more nuanced our appreciation of causality, the more effectively we can achieve the results we want—be it a healthier planet, a more just society, or a happier life.

While some of what we experience in life is the direct result of our efforts, other conditions that affect us are not of our choosing at all. It's much easier to recognize our role in the immediate results of our intentional actions. What is harder is seeing our role in the indirect results of those actions. Marriage, choice of profession—these are conditions that shape a person's life and that she or he directly and knowingly creates. But our actions also have many consequences that we may not have anticipated.

Our actions impact others, directly and indirectly, but they also create conditions that later we must experience ourselves, like it or not. Finding ourselves in situations that we did not choose but that have come about through our previous actions is simply another facet of living within webs of causality that we ignore at our own risk.

As we move through the world, we initiate long series of events, each helping cause the next. A single act impacts a much wider sphere than we generally recognize. Our actions have ripple effects beyond the direct results that we readily perceive and recognize as consequences of our actions. In Buddhism, we often use the language of *karma* to describe the relationship between intentional actions and their full range of results. However, it is not necessary to apply such terms to understand that due to interdependence, everything we do has an impact not only on us and on our immediate surroundings but far beyond that.

Widening our scope of vision is essential if we are to understand and fully appreciate the more subtle workings of causality. Our initial focus may be on our immediate surroundings and the way in which interdependence affects us personally, as an individual. But to fully appreciate the role of interdependence in shaping our world and our experience of it, we need to develop an awareness of causes and effects, actions and reactions, in a greatly expanded context.

WIDENING THE LENS

Living with a sense of this wider horizon is necessary for us to thrive both as a global society and as individuals. Many problems arise when we limit our view to a narrow, self-centered focus. Selfishness acts as a kind of close frame, limiting and distorting our view of reality.

Our grasping at what is *me* and *mine* puts up walls that can make our world close in on us. We end up peering out through narrow windows and seeing what goes on around us through a myopic lens. No wonder there is such a sense of alienation and loneliness in the world. Opening up to the view of interconnectedness helps us to break down the barriers erected by our own egocentrism and to emerge from the narrow and dark cell in which we tend to shut ourselves away.

The wisdom that arises when we fully comprehend our interdependence is a force that can dismantle the walls that separate us from others. Compassion, or an altruistic outlook, can have the same effect. Wisdom and compassion can grow from the awareness that we are all absolutely equal in our wish for happiness and in our longing to be free of pain and suffering. Any being that has the capacity to feel pain merits our respect and our concern. Our recognition of this shared yearning can itself awaken a concern for the well-being of another. When we feel it fully as part our very being, then we will naturally act to alleviate the pain of others and add to their happiness. As such, our vivid awareness that all living beings are perfectly equal in terms of their shared yearning for happiness can be fundamental in reorienting us as we live our interdependence.

In this way, we first need to broaden our awareness. A central aim of this book is to help awaken that awareness and translate it into feelings that lead to action. To truly feel our interdependence, we need a genuine change of heart. Just gathering information about our personal problems or the social ills facing us is of limited benefit. We can see this in the case of the warnings that are printed on cigarette packages. The package clearly informs us that smoking kills, yet it is equally clear that this knowledge has not deterred the billion people around the world who still smoke. This is what happens when our knowledge remains as bare information, without deeply felt insight or concern.

People used to argue that smoking is a matter of personal choice, since smokers only harm themselves. But when researchers looked more closely at effects, they discovered that smokers also harm those around them, through secondhand smoke. The narrow lens makes self and others seem wholly disconnected, but when we widen it we see that our actions affect others and others' actions affect us.

TO BENEFIT OR HARM

Interdependence reveals that the pursuit of our aims can either benefit or harm others, directly or indirectly. Because of interdependence, our actions affect others inevitably and can either contribute to their well-being or impact them adversely. As we pursue our own happiness, we have a responsibility to consider the impact of our actions on others' welfare.

You may recall the terrible disaster that occurred in Bangladesh in 2013 when a factory building collapsed. Similar tragedies have happened all over the world, but this took place during the meetings that led to this book and served as a vivid illustration. Day by day, we watched the death toll climb painfully as people searched desperately through the rubble. In the end more than 1,100 people lost their lives. The people in this building had been producing clothing for large international companies. Most who died were women, and some had their children with them while they worked. The structure appears to have been poorly built in the first place and was not properly maintained subsequently, to save costs and increase profit margins.

International companies have their clothes assembled in Bangladesh, China, and other places where they can avoid offering the salaries and healthy working conditions that people with a higher standard of living can demand. This is in turn because enough people in the United States, Europe, and other affluent communities are willing to purchase their clothes at a cheap price no matter what labor conditions they were produced under. The choice of which clothing you buy may seem to be a personal choice, but in this case it entails importing your own comfort by exporting disaster and suffering to others elsewhere.

To fulfill our responsibilities as members of a global society, it is crucial we look beyond immediate consequences and consider the indirect implications of our conduct. For with our individual actions, we impact the lives of others and shape the world that is our common home.

CUMULATIVE ACTION, CUMULATIVE EFFECTS

We not only share the world; many of us also share similar attitudes and behaviors. When enough people think and act in similar ways, the effect of those actions is amplified. We can refer to this dynamic as *cumulative action* or *collective action*. In Buddhist terms we call this *collective karma*, which in this case simply refers to the fact that many people engaging in the same intentional action has a cumulative effect that impacts us all.

We do not generally spend much time thinking about the wider impact of our collective actions and attitudes. When we can see the immediate results of our personal actions, we take more care. But the connection between collective actions or shared attitudes and their longer-term or indirect impact is more obscure, and for this reason we fail to concern ourselves with these wider consequences.

The world has always been interdependent. But in the twenty-first century, communications technologies help make that fact more readily visible to us. Globalization promotes—and global society seems to be embracing wholeheartedly—a consumer culture that is spread instantly through communications technologies. This lends an added force to shared attitudes and actions. Our individual lifestyle choices are greatly amplified as consumer trends and values are expressed online and carried rapidly to all corners of the globe. More and more people seek to embrace the global consumer culture they see articulated online, believing such a lifestyle will bring them personal happiness and social success.

We urgently need to recognize that we are not making choices for ourselves alone. When we choose for ourselves, we are also choosing for many others. Therefore we need to take much greater care what we decide and how we behave. Many individuals acting out of personal wants and desires have far-reaching collective effects on the world as a whole.

NO PERSONAL STREETS

As just one example, look at the use of motor vehicles in our cities. When I first arrived in India fourteen years ago, there were cars on the road in Delhi, of course, but traffic by and large flowed. Today, however, the city is notorious for its traffic jams, and you can spend a great deal of time in the car without moving. Some reports put the current number of registered vehicles in Delhi at five million.

How did there come to be so many cars on the road? It is often as simple as one person buying a new car and their neighbor feeling that they, too, ought to have one. But the choice to purchase a car is not a purely personal matter, however much it may appear so to the individual consumer. When we are buying a car, we behave and think as if we were acting in a vacuum. We consider what kind of car we want and can afford, weigh our own preferences for color and style, and then just go ahead and buy it without widening our perspective.

But when it comes time to put the car on the road, we have a rude awakening. We discover that our personal car did not come with its own personal streets to drive on. Once we find ourselves stuck in a traffic jam because everyone else is also trying to drive down the same road, the thought may occur to us that we are not acting alone.

Imagine if everyone in your city bought a car, and a flood of cars sat stagnant in the streets. They would have to stack the cars one on top of another! There would be piles of people sitting in their cars waiting for the government to better regulate and fund other options for transportation. As we grumble about the inconvenience, it is important to see that our own failure to consider the cumulative impact of our actions is actually a major part of the problem.

DEVELOPING INNER RESOURCES

Such visible signs of our interdependence can be observed all around us. But as I have been urging, we must not limit our awareness of interdependence to such external displays. We can see the causality of interdependence very much at work internally as well. Our interdependent lives are shaped not only by material conditions but also by our emotional states, by the strength of inner qualities like patience, love, or wisdom, and by the beliefs and perceptions that influence our decisions—in short the whole suite of cognitive and affective forces at work within us.

When I speak of the inner world, I do not have in mind an inner world that is totally distinct from the outer world. However, between our outer and inner conditions, I would argue that these inner conditions have more influence in shaping our world than the outer. This is because our inner world is constantly shaping the way we perceive and respond to the circumstances we find ourselves in. How do external situations appear in your mind? Is your mind disturbed? Do you feel happy? Your inner world has a powerful role in determining how you experience your external conditions and respond to them. There are people whose external conditions appear to be fine or even great, yet they may be holding sadness and experiencing a great deal of darkness within. Conversely, some who live in seemingly abject circumstances may experience contentment and joy.

We have within us already the most important resources we need for living interdependence well. We have tremendous mental flexibility that allows us to adopt new positions in relation to changing circumstances. As I will explore in the following chapters, I believe that we have the basic ability to open our hearts to others, to take their perspectives into consideration, and to share experiences and feelings. Our natural capacity for empathy is a clear sign that we are emotionally connected. If one child cries, another will cry. When people are wholeheartedly laughing, we often cannot help but join in, even if we do not know what is funny. These are all small signs that we are connected inwardly and not just outwardly.

Focusing on our inner interdependence allows us see that we are all moved by the same inner drive to seek happiness and avoid suffering. This universal wish motivates life on this planet. The happiness we all seek only comes when we are working not just on external conditions but on inner ones as well.

THE INTERPLAY OF INNER AND OUTER WORLDS

Far from existing in isolation from one another, in fact, the outer material world and our inner world actively impact one another. Our inner conditions have an enormous impact on the outer world. Our attitudes and feelings, for instance, affect those around us emotionally. More broadly, our emotions incline us to behave in certain ways. Our attitudes also shape our actions, and with our actions we are creating the world we all share.

Conversely, our external conditions also shape us inwardly. Sometimes it looks to me as if modern society has come to be like a machine, one that we are all part of and move through like automatons. There can seem to be little warmth. Due to this lack of love, we come to feel isolated and lonely. This is a sign that the outside world is affecting us. We can be surrounded by people, and clearly be connected in various ways, but we feel as if the inside and the outside are far apart. In fact, they are not. They are interacting, but because we have not correctly learned how to live our interdependence well, we fail to see and feel this.

The primary resources we need to thrive in our interdependent world are inner ones. Usually if we lack something in terms of our material conditions, we feel deprived and experience ourselves as lacking. Even when we have ample material resources, this does not guarantee a state of inner well-being, and besides, they can be taken from us at any time. But if it is possible to feel content whether we have much or little, which set of resources is more valuable: mental and emotional, or physical and material?

WHAT INTERDEPENDENCE FEELS LIKE

The term that I have been using—interdependence—is the most common English translation of a Tibetan term that might also be translated as "interconnectedness."

Thinking of our deep relatedness as interconnection might help it appear less threatening. Connection evokes something we choose, whereas dependence does not. The notion of dependence may sound a bit as if, like it or not, you have been cast into a position of dependence. We do not like to think of ourselves as dependent. "Interconnected" sounds more desirable. We want to connect, and we recognize connectedness as something positive. We may feel more inclined to embrace our basic condition when we think of ourselves as being interconnected rather than interdependent. With that in mind, this book has the title *Interconnected*, to help encourage a positive engagement with our profound relatedness to others and to the world.

When it comes to relationships with people for whom we feel affection—such as parents or friends—then the dependence in our interdependent relationship can seem comfortable or even pleasant. We feel we have someone we can trust and lean upon. Our reliance upon them is a source of well-being and happiness. But when we are cast into the position of dependence on others unwillingly, we experience that quite differently.

Actually, we have a choice. We can either experience our inescapable interdependence as a comforting sense of connectedness, or we can resist it as a form of compulsion and unwanted dependency. It depends on our attitude. But however we may choose to name it, we are all connected, and we depend and rely upon one another in different ways. The element of interdependence and interconnectedness is part and parcel of all our relationships. The choice lies not in whether to be interconnected but in how we live it.

I can imagine that this reorientation from our vision of ourselves as independent to interdependent can be jarring. You might wonder, for instance, how we can exercise personal freedom. How can we make our own choices and stand on our own two feet if we are subject to this interdependence with others? The question of how we can assert self-determination within an interdependent world is an important one, and we will be exploring it throughout the chapters below.

OUR INTERDEPENDENT INDIVIDUALITY

Put simply, we can see ourselves as independent individuals or we can acknowledge our interdependence on one another and on the planet. A great deal is at stake in which of these two views—individualism or interdependence—we choose to adopt. We experience our lives differently, we relate to others differently, and the very society we create differs based on whether we believe ourselves to be fundamentally separable and independent, or fundamentally connected and interdependent.

It is not that one of these two paradigms is absolutely bad and the other good. However, I feel that greater opportunities derive from seeing ourselves as interdependent, or interconnected.

In the end, the individualistic view places more limits on us than interdependence. When we experience ourselves as interconnected in infinite ways to others, we have many options as to how we can relate. By contrast, adopting individualism as our path in life leads us to compare our personal situation to that of other individuals, as if we were separate entities. In such comparisons, one or the other always comes up short. We then end up striving to make sure we are not on the losing end of the comparison.

Such comparisons with others are endless. We see a person with more wealth and feel a desire to be like them—to have a phone like theirs or a car like theirs. Instead of listening within to see what we truly need or want, we focus more on trying to keep up with others. We feel a lack, and we become boxed in by a sense of inadequacy. This unnecessary pressure to measure up keeps us at war with ourselves, either wanting to fit in or to stand out. We come to feel that the relative differences in wealth reflect essential differences in our fundamental worth.

In reality, no one is absolutely poor or rich. Like short and long, rich and poor are relative terms, gaining meaning as a result of juxtaposing different things. They have no fixed meaning in and of themselves. Nothing is inherently or absolutely short or long, and likewise no one is inherently rich or poor. In other words, the ideals we strive to live up to in an individualistic way of life are themselves based on interdependence; they only come to light when we compare things in relationship to each other.

Determining who we are or how we are doing in life by comparing ourselves to others will never give us a stable or reliable measure of our well-being, because comparative judgments always shift based on who we are comparing ourselves to.

We do not need to live our lives measuring ourselves against external standards set for us by others. We do not need to limit ourselves to those options. When we view who we are on the model of interconnectedness, we know that we are no single thing—not a fixed or bounded entity. The options for who we can become are as boundless as the number of points in an open network. Since we are related to all other points, we can strengthen our connections and grow in any direction. We can set our own course in life.

I feel that seeing ourselves as interdependent rather than as separate individuals is more productive because it offers more opportunities for freedom. We do not need to define ourselves by how we stand up to an endlessly moving external measure. Individuality gives a sense of restriction. Interdependence gives a greater sense of possibility.

BRINGING IT TO LIFE

However we choose to live it, interdependence permeates global society and pervades all our own personal interactions with others. It is the basic condition for our survival and for our ability to act in the world. There are many kinds of conditions. Some are optional, while others are necessary. In the case of interdependence, it is a basic, absolutely indispensable condition for our existence.

In this first step, we have been recognizing its presence and understanding how it works. However, the real power of interdependence is not so much as a theory but as a value that guides our life. This deep awareness of our interconnectedness can change our lives and change the world. It can reorient our lives, individually and collectively. It is a project of living in accordance with reality. It moves us from understanding, to feeling, and in the end becomes a springboard to action.

TWO

True Connectivity

W E ARE LIVING in a paradoxical moment. We are technically more connected than at any other point in history, but our technological connectivity itself often leaves us feeling emotionally disconnected or isolated.

Even as we hold in our hands the tools and data to trace patterns of interdependence around the globe, there is still a great distance between what we know of the world and our emotional engagement with that knowledge. We are discovering that we are far more interconnected than we had previously realized, but our way of feeling and living in the world has not caught up with our new understanding.

To close that gap, we can first explore the factors that are obstacles to actually feeling more connected to the world we encounter online. Then we can look for ways to use technological connectivity more wisely so as to take advantage of the opportunities it does offer.

The information we find online tends to stress what is unique or different about people, focusing on disparities in the material conditions of our lives, or on religious and cultural differences. This leads our attention away from what we have in common and can leave us unable to see, let alone feel, our connectedness to people we view on our screens.

Reflecting on your own experiences can help make clear how this works. Chances are you live in a comfortably furnished home, set the temperature exactly as you want it, and open the door any time you like to a refrigerator full of food you enjoy. You can also surf the Internet from a comfortable chair and view images of people who have no homes or whose shelter is made of bits of plastic and cardboard. You can watch videos of their struggle to find enough food and clean water to drink. As you do so, you may feel some pity or sympathy as you observe their plight on the screen, but you are likely to feel that you are looking at them from across a great distance.

A rift opens in our minds, separating us from people whose living conditions differ substantially from ours. When we pay so much attention to the outer conditions that shape people's lives, we end up focusing on what distinguishes us, overlooking what unites us. This can contribute to a sense of distance or separateness from others. The same sense of distance between us and them opens up in the case of people with different cultures and religious backgrounds. I am not speaking here of physical distance but emotional and mental.

Viewing others through the lens of interdependence helps us see that we are not separate from people on the other side of these seeming gaps. We are capable of seeing causal connections that link us to others who appear to be remote from us, even if such links are not visible to the naked eye. For example, we can review the ample evidence and arguments that show that those who have less economic power provide the labor that keeps down the cost of living and fuels the material prosperity of those who have more. This means we can identify ties between our meal and the field workers who harvested our vegetables and factory workers who manufactured our dishes. Yet having this intellectual knowledge of our connection to them does not automatically make us feel personally close to them, especially when the outer conditions of their lives seem so different from our own.

We are in many ways creatures of habit. If we live within certain conditions long enough, they come to seem natural to us. But if we had lived in different conditions, they would seem equally natural. Looking at the cultural, religious, or material conditions that others have become habituated to may make us feel that they must be totally different from us, but we are just mistaking something circumstantial for something essential. It is largely an accident of our birth and our life circumstances that we have come to find certain conditions familiar and others alien or distant. It is not an indication of anything essentially other or different about us.

Beyond any superficial circumstantial factors that differentiate us, all living beings share a much deeper common ground, as I discussed in the previous chapter. Buddhism identifies this deeper ground as the wish to be happy and the longing for freedom from suffering. This fundamental inner condition lies at the very core of our existence. Our apparent physical and circumstantial differences are relatively unimportant and shallow, compared to the more important—and much more foundational—level of reality on which we all stand.

Focusing on this deeper level can help us to access a sense of closeness and shared experience—of all being in it together. With this as our starting point, we can explore our particular conditions without experiencing them as a gulf that separates us.

GOING BEYOND VIRTUAL REALITY

Communications technology has great potential as a tool to bring us closer. The Internet can help us discover that others are like us, and that we are not as alone as we think. It can enable people to connect with others who suffer from similar conditions and find comfort and support in online communities. However, to fulfill the full potential such tools offer, we must use them wisely. Otherwise they can easily end up leaving us further disconnected from one another and from reality.

When topics and events are presented online in a way that highlights what is out of the ordinary, and on top of that receive disproportionate attention, this skews our vision of reality overall. A hypersensitivity to differences desensitizes us to our universal shared condition. Such exaggeration of anomalies can have several harmful effects. One is, as I mentioned, that we can find it hard to identify with people whose experiences we encounter online, because we feel excessively distant and different.

Another is that we end up presenting ourselves as something other than we are when we compete with others in social media. We may be selective about what we share of ourselves in other social contexts as well, but our interactions online are stripped of all the nonverbal clues others use in interpreting what we show of ourselves. The complete lack of direct contact creates a sort of vacuum in which we can easily create an artificial persona. This leads to inauthentic relationships with others, and with ourselves.

In my view, in navigating the online world we need to be very aware of this role of illusion in our virtual connections. This is the case for the information that the Internet delivers but also for the kinds of experiences it offers us. The social aspects of connecting electronically can be especially tricky.

Whether through text messages, sites like Facebook, or other forms of social media, we often reach out because we want someone to talk to and engage with. Yet we are connecting as virtual selves with virtual others, and there are many intermediate layers that we must pass through to "connect" online. When we interact with others online, we do so as an illusory electronic self, interacting with illusory electronic versions of other people.

It is quite strange, really. We see pixels on a screen and hear the digital reproduction of someone's voice, and we think, "I see them, they see me, and we can talk." But when you get right down to it, there is no one there. It is an electronic and therefore artificial representation we are gazing at and talking to. This may be an entertaining way to pass our time, but when we are in real emotional pain, these electronic connections fall far short of the comfort and intimacy we yearn for. It is extremely difficult for technology to transmit the basic human warmth that we all need, and that we especially seek in our moments of pain.

When you are hurt, sometimes you just want someone to hug you. A flat screen cannot hold your hand and share your pain. Even if your loneliness is relieved by a text message or a smiling face on your screen, those data bytes can never fully replace the full vividness of direct contact with someone who is present with you physically and emotionally.

We feel puzzled and saddened when our virtual connections leave us feeling emotionally disconnected, but it is hardly surprising that electronic interactions should be ultimately unsatisfying. Basically we are sitting alone with a screen, hoping to experience authentic closeness. We are carried so far away by the allure of these illusory connections that we end up trapped within our own private world of electronic illusion.

This age of connectivity has the danger of habituating us to an increasingly mediated, virtual form of human engagement. Real life seems to slip further and further from our grasp. I think the sadness and sense of loneliness that is so pervasive today is a sign that we have lost touch with the fullness of human contact. We come to live in a lonely world of illusions that we have created for ourselves. We can spend hours consuming one image after another, sending out one selfie after another, but actually engaging very little with others. The virtual world is absorbing and entertaining, but it is fundamentally illusory and unsatisfying. It is not real or nourishing.

Of course, we might hide behind the facades we present in direct personal encounters too, but it is much easier to construct false appearances from behind an electronic screen. When we fail to differentiate between the illusory forms of mediated connection online and more genuine forms of connection, we are in danger of losing touch with our own inner resources for living interdependence, including our own capacity to be present and to feel authentic closeness to others.

DON'T LIVE A LITE LIFE

In the past, perhaps people could justify actions that had a harmful impact because they didn't have access to the right information. We no longer have that excuse. On the contrary, we have more than enough information. Once we know where to find it online, we already have all that we need to describe in great detail the patterns of interconnectedness that encompass all aspects of life on this planet.

However, as powerful a resource as connectivity can be, and as great a wealth of information as it puts at our disposal, the way we use technology can make it harder for us to make the shift from intellectual to emotional engagement with the world it opens up to us. We now have access to far more information than we can reasonably process. Our response to the sheer volume of information to be found online is often to just surf along the surface of an infinite number of issues and events. We need to go deeper. Knowing more is not a substitute for feeling more.

New technologies are ostensibly introduced to address problems we face and to improve our lives. However, if we do not engage with them in deeper ways, this force that is meant to make our life better all too often can end up making our lives silly. From my point of view, far from truly enriching or nourishing us in any substantial way, our constant connectivity can easily end up trivializing our lives. Our communication of human emotion is reduced to emoticons. When our friends share their joys and pains on Facebook, rather than truly reach out to share those experiences with them, we click "Like" and might not even add a personal comment before we move on to another page. We may think communications technology is adding spice and flavor, but in the end it can detract from the meaning and purpose of our lives, making our lives *lite*.

When I look at its place in our lives today, I often feel that technology is using us, rather than us using technology. For this reason, it is important for each of us to look carefully at our own personal use of technology or, more to the point, look at how our use of technology impacts us. We can start by asking ourselves: "What does it do to me to engage with technology in this way? How does it actually make me feel? What benefits do I expect to gain? What am I willing to give up in order to gain those benefits?"

We focus so intensely on the screen in front of us that we lose our perspective and greatly exaggerate its importance as a source of our happiness. We have the unrealistic assumption, which we seem to really believe, that we can find happiness in screens or in other external objects around us.

This is just not true. Happiness in life does not come back at us from the things around us. It can only be found within us and emanate out from there. As long as we look to technology—or anything else outside us, for that matter—to meet our unrealistic expectations for happiness, we only end up with another problem to solve. Worse, it can lead us further away from actual reality, and from a wholesome, natural life. We begin to live virtual lives instead of actual lives.

EMOTIONAL DISCONNECTIVITY

Many of my friends have commented to me that they often feel emotionally disconnected even though they are almost constantly interacting online. Technological connectivity seems completely natural to those who have grown up with it, but at the same time it remains deeply dissatisfying. Even though people are already communicating with one friend, they say they still feel an urge to connect with someone else, by text or social media. It is confusing to feel so disconnected when your life is so full of connectivity. But there is a reason.

I myself grew up very differently—as far from connectivity as you can possibly get. In the sparsely populated part of the Tibetan plateau where I grew up, there were absolutely no electronics of any sort. Even if we had received any appliances, there was no electricity to plug them into. I am not sure anyone in the family had so much as a wristwatch. Perhaps my father had one, but certainly no one else in the family did. The schedule of our day was not determined by what any clock could tell us. We were attuned to the natural rhythms of life and to our natural surroundings. If we wanted to get a sense of where we were in the day, we looked at the sun and the length of the shadows.

Our labor was not driven by the hour of the day but by the actual work needing to be done. When my father had some task that required his attention, he went to do it. When my mother had work to do, she did it. When there were chores that we children were asked to help with, we tended to them. With no modern conveniences, and a good number of animals to look after, there was plenty of work to do, but this natural way of relating to work left ample opportunity for us to simply be together. When there was no labor we needed to engage in, we did not try to keep busy by finding something else to occupy our time. Rather, we spent whatever time we had free together, talking, telling stories, drinking tea, and generally enjoying each other's company. There was a tangible warmth and feeling of closeness. This way of life was deeply satisfying on a basic human level.

Of course, that was a pastoral way of life—basically a premodern lifestyle. My early life probably seems like another world to you, and sometimes it does to me, too. In one sense, the place I lived in was so remote that it can seem like I also lived in a remote time. In fact, it was just two decades ago that I left there, but that way of life has already been all but extinguished.

In our modern world it is typical that the father goes out to work, the mother goes out to work, and the children go to school. Everyone follows his or her own schedule, and seldom is everyone home at the same time. Even just sitting down to eat together at the same table is a rarity. Family members stay in touch by sending one another text messages. The mother texts the father. The children communicate with their parents by text too.

This really is a bit funny, isn't it? Even within the same household, more communication may be done electronically than face to face. People send texts to one another from one part of the house to another, or even while they are sitting together in the same room. What this means is, you are together but you are not really together.

Whenever you connect to the screen, you are disconnecting from everything in your actual surroundings. You are not really present where you are. Your focus is continually directed somewhere else, toward people who are physically absent. In this way, you too become absent to the people around you, even though you are right there next to them. There is no longer anything natural about this way of being with others.

Connectivity has given us many advantages, but it often comes at the significant cost of losing our natural way of being with others. Losing the ability to be fully present when we are with others can have a devastating effect on our relationships and keeps us constantly out of step with reality. This is a terribly high price to pay for our online activity. Even if we have no intention of reducing our electronic communications, at the very least we should be taking this hidden personal cost into consideration when deciding how we want to use our various devices.

We can see that emotional connections have become terribly shallow, and fundamentally unsatisfying. Unfortunately, this all too easily becomes a self-perpetuating cycle. Because you feel dissatisfied with the shallow connections you have, you look to add more and more. You go online to try to find more friends, or exchange text messages with more people, in the hopes that somehow filling your time with more of this type of connection will make you less lonely. But when the quality of each connection is fundamentally shallow, increasing the number of them just brings more dissatisfaction. Many empty connections still comes up empty.

Worse, it is especially distressing to feel lonely when you apparently have so many friends. But if you are looking for a sense of closeness, what you need is to connect directly with real friends, not connect virtually with more Facebook friends. You need to extend your heart to others, not just extend your fingertips to a keyboard.

INTRODUCING HIS LONELINESS

I know what loneliness feels like. Many people use the title His Holiness to refer to me, but I sometimes joke that His Loneliness would be more accurate. In my own case, although I do not connect to people online, I do have lots of people surrounding me all day long, supporting me in different ways, as well as other people coming to see me. It would seem I should never be lonely. However, I am seen as the reincarnation of a 900-year-old historical figure. In traditional Buddhist terms, the Karmapa is a lofty figure, on a par with the Buddha. People who view me in this way expect me to be a mind reader, a miracle worker, and perfect in every way. When they look at me, this is quite often what many people believe they are seeing. Forget about being on a pedestal, I am practically expected to float in the sky!

For so holy and exalted a personage, it is a little complicated to go about finding friends. Who wants to be friends with someone who is considered to be not entirely human? In terms of social media like Facebook, I am a public figure. This means I can have only a following and *likes*, but I cannot have *friends*. In any case, someone else maintains my presence on social media. If I wanted to connect with my friends on social media, I would need to use a pseudonym, which would be unethical for me. In any case, posing as someone else defeats the whole purpose of a real friendship.

I know that my life situation is unusual, to say the least, but we all have to deal with unrealistic expectations that others project onto us. Such projections can leave us feeling isolated and prevent us from being seen for who we really are.

Sometimes consciously but often not, we ourselves actively project an illusory online self onto social media and other virtual platforms. It is more typical for people to post pictures or stories of themselves when they are happy than when they are feeling distressed. The virtual world does not generally encourage us to share our vulnerable side. Since everything we post is judged by the number of likes and retweets or shares, we are selective in what we expose of ourselves. Even when we post about our problems, we might do so in a way that leaves us free of apparent responsibility for those problems, so we can appear as victims and elicit sympathy. We learn to market ourselves. As a result, the electronic version of ourselves is a distorted and packaged self. This is another significant obstacle to authentically connecting with others through electronic media.

Loneliness is not solely a product of our use of technology. There are many other conditions, inner and outer, that contribute to our feeling that way. With such heavy emphasis on being self-reliant and standing on our own two feet, people resist leaning on others and can end up feeling very lonely. The fact is, we all rely on others in different ways. Why should we deny it? We place so much value on individuality and independence, it seems as if wanting to be close and feel connected to others is embarrassing or an insult to one's dignity.

One difference I have observed between Tibetan and Western contexts is that people raised in Western cultures tend to be less comfortable acknowledging that they need help. If an elderly Tibetan is having a hard time standing up, he or she warmly appreciates being lent a hand to get up. In fact, not to do so might be considered impolite or selfish. In the West, if you reach out to help, you run the risk of embarrassing or insulting the elderly person, as if you were implying that they are incapable of getting up on their own.

When people are urged to see themselves as autonomous and independent, loneliness is more common. Learning to live as an interdependent human being can help overcome your sense of loneliness. When you are emotionally aware of your interconnectedness, you will know you are never truly alone.

Loneliness is not just a result of your outer physical or social situation. If mentally or emotionally you feel alone, it does not matter how many thousands of others flock to you, as I know from personal experience. Nor is the experience of loneliness the result of a single cause or a single condition but of numerous ones. Therefore it cannot be completely resolved by one single cause or condition. But accepting the undeniable fact of your own interdependence, and learning to work with it, is a powerful condition that can help bring about a shift.

COME IN FROM THE COLD

To ease loneliness we first need to find friends within ourselves. We can start by connecting with our own positive qualities, such as love and compassion. We can learn to treasure and value these inner qualities and draw our strength from them first and foremost. These qualities are our inner conditions for interdependence and are our closest and most reliable allies in negotiating the outer conditions of our interdependence.

Within each of us there is a deep well of potential goodness—of radiance and nobility. The problem is that we do not always know how to draw from this well or make it a source of ongoing sustenance and support.

You could think about it this way: Perhaps when you feel lonely, it is actually your positive qualities that are lonely. It could be your goodness that has become surrounded by adverse factors, unhealthy habits, and cold attitudes. You can surround your own lonely potential for goodness instead with supportive factors and warm attitudes. You can become a friend to your basic radiance and wholeheartedly, unequivocally nurture your own positive qualities. This can bring a quality of warmth and richness to your time alone. Even if no one else is around you, you can experience connection rather than isolation.

If you know that you harbor within you kind thoughts and good-hearted feelings, that itself can be enough. If you lose heart just because no one else sees it, this is a sign you yourself do not truly appreciate the value of your positive thoughts and feelings. You need to delight in them yourself, and be heartened by their presence within you. You can actively appreciate them and feel that they make your existence meaningful. You more than anyone else have the resources to warm yourself from within.

You should not put yourself out in the cold and then resent others for leaving you there. You can warm your own heart from within. You can draw on your own inner resourcefulness. It is not realistic to expect people to see into your heart and approve what is there. In any case, it is this warm and wholesome part of yourself—this inner strength—that you need to draw forth so that friends can connect with it. It is this part of yourself that allows you to enter into warm and healthy relationships with others. It is these inner qualities that enable you to feel your connections of interdependence and flourish in them.

When we are trying to cultivate a capacity to feel closeness to others, we do not need to create anything new. We are cultivating a latent ability, albeit one that might have been neglected or impaired during the course of our lives. There is every indication that the ability to experience genuine closeness is an innate potential of all human beings.

Infants and young children naturally and spontaneously reveal what they feel. They are not held back by inhibitions or enmeshed in habits of deception. One effect of babies' naturalness is that people feel affection toward them, and this kindness that others show them is necessary for their survival. We find small children adorable and loveable, and we are therefore willing to take care of their needs. People stop to admire them and want to caress and hold them. If they cry, we want to discover why so we can give them whatever they lack. When humans are very young, we are naturally open and straightforward. If a small child sees another playing at something, he or she might walk straight up and join the other in the play. Children unselfconsciously wave at people in passing trains or cars. They do not doubt others' intentions or seek to deceive them.

The impulse to connect arises naturally in human beings, as is clearly visible in us when we are children. Later, as we become adults, this ability is eroded by doubts, fears, and suspicions. For example, if there are two families living in an apartment building and each has a young child, the parents might pass each other in the lobby without exchanging a single word or even making eye contact, but the children will undoubtedly acknowledge each other when they meet. If a small child in front of the building spots another at a window on an upper floor, she may spontaneously wave, and the other child will wave back.

I have heard of a research study done on interaction in elevators between strangers, both human and chimpanzee. An adult human was told to take the elevator to the ground floor. On their way down, the elevator stopped on an intervening floor and another person stepped in and pressed the button for another intervening floor. The person in the elevator first often displayed agitation and certainly had no smile or word of greeting to spare for the person slowing them down in this way, even though they were sharing a small space. Yet when the experiment was done with two chimpanzees, when the chimpanzees suddenly found themselves in the same elevator, they expressed delight at meeting another of their kind and joyfully embraced one another. The human beings were also meeting another of their kind and, even more than chimpanzees, were equipped with the capacity to recognize that fact. We humans have so much in common and easily feel connected when we are young. But we often do not manage to retain the ability to feel spontaneously close to others as we grow older.

In terms of our nature—our constant yearning to be happy and to be free of suffering—we are profoundly the same and close. Yet through habituation and conditioning, we grow distant. We invest tremendous importance in our differences—our different beliefs, different cultural assumptions, and different identities. We cover our sameness up with layers of difference. No wonder we then find it hard to connect and feel close, although a wish to connect is grounded deep in our being.

What can we do to protect and enhance our innate ability to connect with others? I will talk later about strengthening our basic empathy, but I also think that connecting and staying connected with our own good qualities is a powerful step we can take to be able to feel close to others.

What's more, we are always surrounded by others, and connected to others, including people we do not see and will never meet but who have contributed to who we are. Reflecting on interdependence and consciously training ourselves to identify it at work in our lives allows us to cultivate an awareness of others' presence as part of us.

RECOLLECTING KINDNESS

Learning to recognize and feel the kindness of others is a practical measure we can apply to bring our lives more in line emotionally with the intellectual understanding of interdependence. One method that I think could be effective in this regard is taught in Buddhism, but it does not require any faith in Buddhism and can be done by anyone. Called *recollecting kindness*, this practice entails deliberately calling to mind situations in which we recognize that we received something from others. We then consciously turn those instances over in our minds so as to intensify our awareness of others' kindness, until we are filled with a sense of gratitude.

We are surrounded by endless examples of kindness that we could use in this practice. As I have noted, the food we eat, the clothes we wear, and all that we consume comes from others. If we just look at the clothes we are wearing right now, each piece has a distinct history, and those histories connect us very palpably to others. We know without a doubt that our clothes are the result of a great deal of human effort. In all likelihood each item of clothing was made from various materials produced in different places that were all then delivered to a factory where they were sewn together. Many different individuals were involved, some planting and harvesting the cotton, shearing the sheep, or producing the synthetic fibers, others designing the clothes, transporting the fabric, and still others operating the machines, laboring under what in many cases are unhealthy and mind-numbing conditions.

When we put on clothes, we are accepting their kindness in toiling to make the clothes that form part of our well-being. We have not visited the fields, factories, or warehouses, and we have not seen their faces, but we can acknowledge the benefit we have gained from their efforts and feel gratitude for that kindness.

In order to make your sense of closeness more vivid, you could take a further step in connecting to the people who have benefited you from afar. You could take a look at the labels on the clothes you are wearing to see where they were made. Taking advantage of the easy access to information and images that the Internet affords you, you can investigate to actively educate yourself about working conditions and the experiences of factory workers in the place your clothes were made. Do not wait for news of their lives to reach you. Extend yourself and connect with them. Do this with the awareness that, no matter how different the backdrop of their lives appears, just like you they yearn to be happy and free of suffering.

This does not require dramatic action on your part; it just means intensifying your sense of personal involvement. Take the initiative to seek out information, and then merge what you learn with your feelings. This is a way to use the Internet wisely, to allow you to feel your connectedness. You could read about the daily lives of people in that country. You could do a search for images of factory workers. When you find them, look into their eyes, and reflect that they or someone like them ran the machine that sewed your garments. You could learn more about the circumstances of their lives, and try to feel how your life would be if you had grown accustomed to living under those conditions.

When it is grounded in gratitude and a sense of closeness, your greater awareness of the disparities between your living conditions and theirs could motivate you to act to improve their circumstances. At a minimum, each time you put on an article of clothing, you can recognize that you are wearing a sign of others' kindness. You could feel as close to others as your clothes are to you.

When you engage in this sort of exercise with your clothes or anything else, even if the people themselves do not hear your expression of thanks or gain anything from you immediately, under the right conditions your gratitude and sense of closeness to them could lead to action that benefits them. Your feeling of closeness to them can move you to act. You might contribute to organizations that are working to benefit them. You could investigate to see which companies have a serious commitment to ethical labor practices or environmental responsibility. You could decide to avoid purchasing products from countries that lack regulatory protection for their workers. Thanks to the Internet, these are steps you can take from where you are seated right now.

It could inspire you to take greater interest in labor conditions in that place, or to be more conscious of the impact of your consumer choices overall. If there is ever news of natural disasters or political strife in that country, you will take greater interest because of the personal involvement you generated.

If you have the conditions to do so, you might be moved to take this further. You could determine to travel to that country and meet people there. I have met quite a few people who became interested in the Tibetan cause and actually came to India to learn more about the conditions of Tibetans living here in India.

In any case, your experience of closeness to someone who suffers injustice could move you more generally to take action to bring positive change to the world in other ways. After all, improving the world improves their world, too.

Through this intentional exercise in recollecting the kindness of others, two conditions come together—the service others provided you with their labor, and your own conscious cultivation of gratitude—to create a force that leads you to act to benefit those who have benefited you. This is how you can generate the right inner conditions to match your outer conditions of interdependence, to live your interdependence in ways that bring goodness both to yourself and others.

Gratitude is a value of interdependence. It is an inner orientation that aligns us emotionally with the outer reality of our lives. Bringing heart and mind together, gratitude is an affective state that can be produced by an awareness of interdependence. We identify interdependence at work and train ourselves to respond to that awareness with gratitude. Like other values of interdependence, gratitude can lead us from awareness to feelings and, eventually, can culminate in action.

Even setting aside what it inspires you to do for others, when you cultivate gratitude, you certainly gain a great deal yourself in terms of well-being and happiness. When you feel grateful, you recognize that you are the beneficiary of others' kindness. You feel fortunate. Gratitude just feels good, and it can be extended in all directions, since not only clothes but every single thing you use comes to you from others. At mealtime, you can feel grateful for each and every ingredient on your plate, for those who did the cooking and the planting, even for sunlight, for rainfall, and for the minerals that enrich the soil.

You can train yourself in this way to feel surrounded on all sides by goodness and benefit. Everything and everyone is benefiting you. The whole world becomes your personal benefactor and is part of you. You have not only been benefited in material terms. Those whose ideas you find useful, who bring out the best in you, who challenge you to grow—they are also your personal benefactors and form part of who you are.

Teaching yourself to see and feel in this way will make it much easier for you to feel close to others. It can make a tremendous contribution to your personal happiness and can certainly make you a more positive force in the interdependent world.

We can also experience a sense of closeness and connectedness to animals or to nature. I think the feelings of closeness we have toward the earth or to animals can be qualitatively the same as what we feel toward other human beings. In fact, it might actually be easier for us to feel close to animals or nature, precisely because we have made human relationships so complicated. Like human babies, animals are genuinely straightforward and authentic. Animals do not play the manipulative games that adult human beings have become so adept at playing with one another. They do not engage in that sort of pretense. We can train ourselves to shake the habits of deception and manipulation that creep into our human relationships, but this will take a conscious and concerted effort. With animals, we can experience that naturally, right now. For many people, their relationship to a pet can serve as an important source of closeness and love.

Many of us are moved when we see how animals behave and how they care for one another. Videos of interspecies interactions have some of the most views on the Internet. I myself enjoy watching them as well. Perhaps these videos reflect our own yearning to be able to connect across our differences. Millions of people might share a video of a dolphin and a whale playing together or a cat mothering an abandoned chick. There is something in this that fascinates us.

When we watch such videos, we marvel at animals' abilities to act against what we assume is their self-serving or self-protective impulses. We can let ourselves be inspired by their natural display of the same inner qualities we would like to cultivate.

Yet for all the ease with which we connect and feel close to our pets and other animals, we all too often remain indifferent to the suffering of animals in general. As we smile at our pet's antics or admire the qualities other animals display in the videos we enjoy so much, I think it would be good to reflect on our impact on the lives of animals more broadly. Many animals suffer terribly because they are put to work for our pleasure and comfort, or are raised for slaughter to satisfy our appetite for their flesh. We are able to be tender and loving toward the pet who sits at our side and yet be causing unbearable pain to the animals whose meat sits on our plate. We find this thought distasteful, and so we mentally distance ourselves by not tracing out the chains of causality and interdependence that link our bite of meat to the distress and terror of animals crowded together in narrow cages or filthy cattle yards. Our own taste for meat is a condition that makes us complicit in a chain of causal actions that results in suffering that we would never stomach if we had to watch it. That suffering is caused by us human beings and is rooted in our failure to recognize our connectedness to those beyond our immediate field of vision.

The same is true of our natural environment. Our clinging to a sense of ourselves as separate individuals, and the selfish behavior it enables, blinds us to our intimate connectedness to the environment. The devastation of our natural environment clearly reflects a failure to appreciate its tremendous value and importance. In the case of our planet, the need to develop feelings of closeness is particularly acute, because we can now all see the devastating effects of exploiting the earth as if it were a lump of rock that has no relationship to us. There might be many other habitable planets in the universe or in other galaxies, but they are of no benefit to us. It is this planet that we need to keep habitable.

Essentially the same problem arises, whether it is in our relationship to other human beings, to animals, or to the planet—and the solution is also the same: cultivating a much broader awareness of the chains of causality that link us to others, and cultivating the feelings of closeness that can inspire us to act.

THREE

Being an Interdependent Individual

THE CONCEPT OF INTERDEPENDENCE may seem jarring when we first apply it to ourselves personally. Sometimes when people first hear the idea that they are interdependent, they think that this somehow negates their individuality. This is far from the case. Our individuality is not threatened by interdependence. On the contrary, it is interdependence that has allowed us to develop the personality traits that define us in unique ways.

As I mentioned earlier, although the idea of being interdependent may be gaining widespread recognition only recently, we have always been interdependent. Nothing has changed in that regard. Nor is there any conflict between being an individual and being interdependent. The contradiction lies in the gap between our assumptions about how we exist as individuals and how we actually exist, namely as interdependent individuals. The only contradiction is between reality and our view of reality.

The notion that each person is a separate, self-sustaining or independent entity is a deeply held assumption. It may seem so self-evident that you have never even questioned it. However, this view of a person as an independent individual is not found in all philosophies or religious worldviews. This idea of a bounded, discrete person may be the most pervasive, but it is certainly not the only way to see things.

There are those who assert that this concept of an autonomous and independent individual is especially a product of the modern West. Yet, however much global society has built on it today, this concept did not originate in modern times or in any single cultural context. When the Buddha taught interdependence over two millennia ago, he did so precisely because he saw that people were clinging to an unexamined assumption that we are all independent and ultimately separate. The Buddha pointed to that deeply held and widespread view as the source of our deepest confusion in life and the gravest problems in society. This shows that the assumption that we are separate and autonomous has a long history and deep roots. It has also had widespread—and harmful—consequences for society and for our personal happiness.

Seeing ourselves as fundamentally separate and independent inclines us to underestimate or altogether ignore the connections between ourselves and others. As happens in our use of electronic connectivity, we feel that we are here, while everyone else is over there, apart from us. We even imagine that we can do whatever we wish with no consequences for anyone but ourselves. Given the environmental impact of our consumer-driven global society, I believe we cannot afford to leave unexamined the assumptions that have allowed us to go so far down this road without noticing the collective effects of our individual actions.

We need other possibilities for understanding who we are as individuals. On a personal level, exploring what it means to be an interdependent individual allows us to stop living at odds with reality. As we gain a more realistic understanding of who we are and how we are interconnected, our lives can become much more satisfying and meaningful.

In other words, "interdependent individual" is not a contradiction. Far from being an oxymoron, this term can be a powerful guide leading us to take better charge of our own lives.

We do not need to be aware of our interdependence in order for it to form the basic condition of our existence as individuals. It does not depend on our acknowledgment, nor is it a matter of personal belief or a passing theory. Interdependence describes reality based on empirical observation. We can analyze our own experiences and come to the same conclusions that scientific studies are now also confirming.

As I mentioned, everything that exists has arisen through the concatenation of multiple causes and conditions, and this is true for every individual as well. Nothing comes from a single cause alone but only through the combined presence of numerous conditions, each of which affects the outcomes in some way. It is not as if each individual had one unique cause and one unique condition. As we began to explore in chapter 1, our very body came from our two parents. Its existence depends on the coming together of two individuals. Their union was one condition for us to be conceived, and there are various other conditions that need to be fulfilled before finally our body is produced as a result. The endless flow of nutrients through the umbilical cord and everything that kept our mother alive during the nine months are all indispensable conditions as well. One thing is certain: we ourselves were not present then, arranging for all those conditions to come together.

However autonomous we may feel ourselves to be, we could not even begin our lives without two specific people who therefore are not entirely distinct from or "other" to us. Once born, we eat food from others, learn from others, and are clothed and cared for all our lives by others. Just a few steps of analysis show us how dependent we are upon many, many others for our basic existence. Who we are as individuals emerges as a result of those diverse causes and conditions. We can give a separate name to that result and use that name to identify ourselves throughout life, but that does not mean we are utterly separate or separable from those causes and conditions. It is completely valid to bear a name that distinguishes us, but we invest a reality in that name that goes far beyond its function. We slowly come to believe that what our name points to is wholly separable from everything else. This message is communicated to us in many ways—and we repeat it to ourselves—"You are unique in the world. You are special. There is no one else like you." It is true we are unique, but to the extent that this discourse heightens our sense of ourselves as absolutely distinct and unrelated to others, this perception itself becomes a main condition for our selfishness.

This feeling of standing apart from all else is an illusion. It was constructed by a process of labeling and projecting. If we examine it, we can see that we exaggerate aspects of who we are and label ourselves based on them, building an independent identity for ourselves. In this way, our sense of being separate is created through mental projection. In the end, *I* and *mine* are concepts—labels that we use to describe ourselves. They are not real entities but concepts that point to a separateness not consistent with reality.

However, just because our sense of ourselves as utterly separate is erroneous does not imply that no *I* exists. Of course you do. But you exist connected to and dependent upon many other factors. You are an interdependent individual.

Our clinging to exaggerated concepts of a self-sufficient and autonomous self blinds us to a basic reality that we need to take into account. Why? Because it structures everything we do and are. The unique person we become over the course of our lives is based on the ongoing interplay of interdependent causes and conditions. If we cling to our individuality without appreciating how that individuality is supported by interdependence, we live in a kind of willful blindness. This harms us, and it can also lead to us harming others. For sure, it limits the positive ways we could shape others through our connections to them.

If we hold to the theory that we are entirely independent agents, and can pursue our individualistic aims without considering the context of interdependence, we will be looking at the world with skewed vision.

FROM ARROGANCE TO LOVE

Viewing ourselves through the lens of interdependence brings certain qualities and values into focus. For example, when we hold to a sense of ourselves as utterly independent, we can come to believe and behave as if we were entirely self-made, as if our own individuality called together all the conditions needed to bring us into being. This can lead to false pride and overbearing arrogance, as if we independently created our own individuality and owe nothing to anyone. When we ignore our interdependence, we are disregarding the importance of others to our well-being. We devalue their contributions to who we are. This kind of pride is a symptom of narrow view. It is a harmful delusion that can seriously impair our ability to relate in a healthy way to others.

Interdependence opens up a different—more realistic and therefore healthier—vantage point from which to relate to our individuality. Consider your sense of self from this perspective: It is only the diversity that interdependence offers that makes you unique. You are unique thanks to the variety of interactions and experiences that you have had over the course of your life, and that are only possible because you exist interdependently. A course you took in college, music you listened to with certain friends, a summer vacation that awakened in you a yearning for wider horizons—each experience could form an integral part of you, and each arose only because of your interconnectedness to others. Interdependence gives you far more resources to draw on in your uniqueness and individuality. Interdependence gives you a reason to value what you have received from others.

The world today is sorely lacking in love, and that lack stems in large part from a failure to appreciate the contributions of others to our own well-being. Others did not simply clothe and feed us; they made us who we are as individuals. By training ourselves to recognize the many ways others have contributed to our survival, well-being, and our very identity, we can develop a genuine sense of cherishing and affection toward them, and these emotions are conditions for developing a vivid sense of responsibility. As we come to truly understand ourselves as interdependent individuals, responsibility comes to feel and look very different, as we will explore in a later chapter.

If we are successful in internalizing our awareness of interdependence and allowing it to become deeply felt, we can shift our self-perception so as to actually experience the intimate connections that link us constantly to others and to the planet. We will be able to move beyond knowing that we are dependent upon other people and the natural world to feeling an active sense of love and concern for them.

REAL SELF-RELIANCE

I hope it is clear that interdependence does not undermine your individuality but is what has enabled you to become the unique person you are today. Embracing your interdependence can give your individuality new meaning. The same is true of self-reliance. There are forms of self-reliance that work in harmony with interdependence, and it is precisely these forms of self-reliance that we most need to cultivate. Thinking in terms of interdependence, in turn, provides a firm base for our exercise of healthy self-reliance.

It is on the basis of interdependence that we are able to consciously change course in life and grow in new directions. We are not destined to live out our lives as dictated by the initial set of conditions that first gave us life.

Interdependence means that change is always possible. This is a basic facet of causality: because all things are dependent on causes and conditions for their existence, all things are always open to change. In fact, they are always changing. Causes and conditions are constantly interacting in ways that affect the outcome. If we think of a seed as a cause and a tree as the result, it is clear that one cause alone does not produce a tree. Conditions such as moisture, soil, and warmth are all instrumental in determining its size, strength, and the quality of its branches and fruit. By manipulating any of those conditions, we change the result.

This is why by changing the conditions in our lives—beginning with our inner conditions—we can change our lives. Because they are interconnected, we can change our inner world and our outer circumstances. We just need to identify correctly the conditions that we can and must change; then we change them. In this way, the greater our attentiveness to the workings of interdependence, the more opportunities we have to take charge of our own lives. This is a true form of self-reliance—self-reliance that does not deny the role of other people or external circumstances but rather wisely takes them into consideration.

In order to work with interdependence to bring about change, we must attend to both the inner and the outer: both the experiences within us and all the interactions we have with our social or natural environment. Outer interdependence may be more tangible and thus easier to observe, but in actual fact, inner conditions of interdependence admit of a far richer versatility and variety.

This work of changing the course of our lives is not accomplished by changing a single cause or a single condition. We need to cultivate many inner conditions to bring about real transformation. The potential has been there with us from the beginning, but once we decide we wish to develop that innate potential, we do so by bringing together all the various conditions that enhance whatever quality we want to strengthen, such as our love, our confidence, or our wisdom.

It is important that we gain a clear understanding of how, at whatever level we choose to look, from the universe at large down to the molecular level, everything that interacts serves as a condition affecting the rest of each system. This is just as true for the workings of our mind and heart as it is for physical systems.

It might help to understand the interdependence of our inner emotional or mental conditions through an analogy of how our internal organs work. Here, too, we see interdependence at work. Having two strong lungs is not sufficient. Our lungs must function in close connection with the rest of our respiratory system, our heart, our liver, and all the rest of the interdependent internal organs. Each needs to have a certain level of health, although if one is slightly compromised, others can compensate to a certain degree. But no one organ can keep us alive on its own.

Just as we need to have these physical organs healthy and strong enough to support life within our body, we need various mental and emotional elements to give life to our compassion and the other virtues of interdependence. We need to look after the health and strength of our motivation, as well as our feelings, our understanding, and our perceptions. In this way, we can exercise our self-reliance to develop the qualities we wish to nurture. But we must do this in a way that acknowledges the fundamental principle of interdependence. A will to change is not enough. Our will must interact with other inner elements, and these together ultimately interact with outer conditions to shape our external circumstances.

This may be helpful to keep in mind if at times we find ourselves progressing more slowly than we had hoped. Once we realize that our personalities are not fixed and that we can decide to actively change them, we might become inspired and expect to be able to push ourselves to change rapidly. But compassion and other inner qualities are not solid things that we can just decide to acquire, install, and power on. They do not exist as discrete or unrelated entities but rather need to be cultivated gradually, over time, and in concert with other qualities.

This is precisely because our inner emotional and mental states exist interdependently, in very much the same way an ecosystem does. Our inner potential can be awakened and brought to fulfillment through the interplay of various conditions. Therefore the task of increasing our virtuous qualities implies multiple steps to meet various conditions. This cannot be accomplished simply by wanting it strongly enough.

SELF-CULTIVATION NOT SELF-ABSORPTION

We need to cherish ourselves and care for ourselves wisely. Developing the qualities we have been discussing is precisely a healthy way to cherish ourselves. We bear the primary responsibility for the state of our own minds and hearts. If we do not look after our inner affairs, who can possibly do that for us? In this sense, healthy cherishing and care of ourselves is valuable.

In Buddhism we say that each person must become his or her own protector. Learning to do this is extremely important. It is the basis for us to be able to extend care and protection to others. This second step is even more important. If our learning to protect ourselves does not contribute to our being able to care for others, we all too easily become stuck in a quagmire of self-obsession. Much of the time, this is what happens: we take our care and cherishing of ourselves too far and arrive at outright self-absorption.

This sort of self-cherishing reinforces the mistaken perception that we are autonomous individuals—and this perception causes us a great deal of confusion in life. Unless we are willing to directly challenge our self-absorption and this sort of cherishing, it is unlikely we will be able to live full and healthy lives as individuals in an interdependent world.

Self-absorption hides from view the vast web of relationships within which our life unfolds. Our awareness becomes restricted to *I* and *mine*—a narrow set of direct connections limited to *my* partner, *my* parents, or *my* friends. With this emphasis on me, mine, and I, how easily iPhone, iPad, and My Documents roll off the tongue! Everything we engage with points us back to *I* and *my*.

I sometimes describe *egocentrism* as a prison in which we have shut ourselves away from everyone and everything else. Our ego makes us a prisoner. Only a limited few people or pets matter to us, and only they are allowed entry into our self-made jail. Everyone else is irrelevant, as if the world outside the prison doesn't really exist. Our own egotism and self-absorption act as the wardens that keep us shut off from the rest of the world.

Our own belief that we are inherently separate from everyone else—our view of ourselves as self-sufficient and independent entities—reinforces those walls. Because we ourselves have created this isolation, only we can liberate ourselves from this imprisonment.

Once we have torn down the walls our egocentrism has built up around us—once we are free—there are no more walls. From the perspective of interdependence, our view is so broad that it can take in the entire world. When we take in the whole world, we finally encompass the whole range of our connections, for we are connected ultimately to the whole world. It is important we make our awareness of our connections as expansive as we can, because as we have seen, we are not only affecting others or impacted by them through immediate and direct interactions. Through long chains of causal connections, what we do personally in our own home or neighborhood helps serve as a condition contributing to the happiness or suffering of others in far corners of the globe, and vice versa. On a larger scale, the actions taken by whatever nation we are a citizen of might either be helping others thousands of miles away, or they might be harming them.

Even as we widen our view to look beyond the confines of our own selves, we should not overlook our own experiences. We can start from them and expand outward. As we cease seeing ourselves as unique and separate and become increasingly aware of how much unites us, we become able to learn about others by seeing our own situation clearly.

We can do this, most basically, by reflecting, "I want to be happy. This means that the people connected to me want to be happy." That is what our own wish for happiness indicates to us.

We have a saying in Tibetan that by knowing what hurts your own body, you know what *not* to do to others. Of course we cannot know everything that others are feeling or thinking. But we can take ourselves as an example and know that others have feelings like we do. This does not mean we can ignore our responsibility to educate ourselves about the unique particulars of others' conditions. In fact, we must do that to ensure that we are impacting them positively. Rather, our knowledge of our basic shared inner condition can be the starting point in motivating changes in our actions so that we benefit others and avoid harming them. This shift toward more compassionate action can begin when we take ourselves as an example and know that others have similar feelings. They want to be happy and free of suffering, just like we do. We start from there.

HUMILITY AND CONFIDENCE

As we look to see what personal qualities we could cultivate to become healthier and happier interdependent individuals, we find humility and confidence have a powerful role. This may seem an unusual pairing when we sense ourselves to be autonomous and self-sustaining. However, new possibilities and new directions make sense when we truly view ourselves as interdependent. The compatibility between humility and confidence is one such new possibility.

Our consumerist society thrives on competition and therefore encourages displays of strength. This inclines us to feel we must present ourselves as successful winners. But this not only makes it hard for us to connect authentically, it inclines us to seek positions of superiority over others and to conceal our weaknesses. This in turn makes it harder to address those weaknesses, which is necessary if we are to grow.

Adopting a posture of humility does not mean that you are weak, although people often assume it does. We Tibetans have a particularly odd way to apply the practice of humility. When someone is particularly skilled at something, they take care to present their abilities with great humility. Someone who is very learned in a certain area might be so aware of all there is yet to learn that they say, "I really know very little about this." This is culturally acceptable in a Tibetan context and can even be seen as a signal that the person must really have something worthwhile to say on the topic. Some Tibetan spiritual teachers go to the West and express themselves in this traditional way. However, if the audience does not recognize that this is the expected way to express humility in Tibetan culture, they may reasonably ask themselves why they have come to listen to some Tibetan monk who knows nothing on the topic he is expounding!

Healthy humility is not the same thing as self-abasement. The point is not to abuse or demean our own qualities. Nor is the point to go from the extreme of needing to be the supreme winner to declaring oneself the worst of the worst. Rather, it is to recognize that since everything is relative, there is always room to grow. You are never the absolute best that ever could or will be in a certain area. By the same reasoning, you are never the absolute worst either.

Cultivating humility as part of our efforts to live interdependence can be enhanced by a heartfelt awareness that we are always in a state of development. Because everything arises based upon the coming together of continually shifting conditions, however much or little of a certain positive quality we have, further growth is always possible. Moreover, our positive qualities can be developed without limit. As long as we are human, we can continually keep discovering new potentials.

This is an important tenet in modern science that would serve us well in life, too. Anyone who says they have reached the final end of knowledge is not a true scientist. When good scientists make an important discovery, they do not feel that this means an end to their experiments or exploration.

You may know a great deal but also know that you can still learn from others and from new experiences. Your wisdom shows you that there is always more to learn. This is where a healthy humility keeps open the door to improvement. Pride, by contrast, closes that door. You sit behind that closed door telling yourself you are better than everyone else and have more than anyone else. The egocentric walls that box us in are constructed in just this way.

Reducing our pride does not imply losing confidence—in fact, far from it. There is an important difference between confidence and pride. With pride, we look down on others. We need them to be less for ourselves to be more. Confidence is a virtuous form of pride. You feel able to do good things.

In Buddhism, we call confidence *antidotal pride*. It may look like pride, but confidence serves as an antidote to help us get rid of our limitations. Both humility and confidence are qualities that allow us to grow beyond our limitations while allowing us to live our interdependence well.

Humility can help us to recognize our responsibilities to others; with confidence we feel able to act to fulfill them.

BEING THE BEST EVER

When we think of ourselves as independent rather than interdependent, not only do we feel distinct and separate from everyone else, we also want to stand out. We like to be told by our friends, "You are the best." We tell ourselves, "My parents are the best parents ever. My vacation was the best vacation ever. My friends are the best friends ever." We often get the message that we only really matter if we are unique and special in some way. This quest for a sense of unique individuality places great pressure on us and makes it easy for us to feel that we are not measuring up to others.

The need to stand out would diminish if we better appreciated the value of what we are and have. This is where a third quality that has great value for us as interdependent individuals comes in: contentment. Contentment implies being able to enjoy what you have and what you are, to truly savor and make full use of it.

Life in consumer culture is characterized by dissatisfaction. This is produced through our habit of thirsting after what we lack. This habit—the habit of desire—leads us to disregard what we have already in a continual search for something newer, something shinier and more exalted. In the end, we lose our ability to feel satisfied with who we are or even notice how much we have already.

This persistent sense of dissatisfaction affects our relationships and our own quality of life. You yourself are not good enough. Your partner is not kind enough or good-looking enough. We experience this when we look at our electronics. A new version is always coming out. However, maybe before we buy the new version, we should be sure we have used all the features of the old version. Otherwise we may gain new features when we are not even using half of the features of our old model. This is true of everything in life. We constantly want more and make our happiness a matter of getting more—better than we now have, and more of it.

We would be far better off learning how to enjoy what we already have rather than chasing more things. Some people believe that dissatisfaction is healthy because it ensures that we will keep progressing in life. They suggest that if we allow ourselves to feel content with what we have, we will become complacent and stop all forward motion. But this is not how it works. There is no inherent conflict between feeling content and progressing in our lives.

Being satisfied or content does not mean we stop growing or never gain anything new. It means truly appreciating what we already have. What point is there in always chasing more if as soon as we have it, we just turn our attention to something else beyond our reach? What's more, contentment offers a strong basis for improvement. When there is no recognition or appreciation for what we have, we lack a firm basis to build on. Mere greed for something else is unstable. To counter it, you can consciously cultivate a sense of satisfaction or even wonder for what you already have.

We invest tremendous energy in making happiness unnecessarily complicated. Happiness can be much more simple and natural. Appreciation and joyful gratitude can arise spontaneously, as a natural extension of our full awareness of interdependence.

What we have already is of great value. In Buddhist practice people are encouraged to know, and especially to feel, that just being a human being in itself is amazing. We have a saying in Tibetan to the effect that just by having a precious human life, you are already halfway to your highest goal. We acknowledge that all life is precious, but living as a human being is especially precious, precisely for the opportunities it offers for consciously developing our positive qualities. When our human life is endowed not only with these opportunities but also with a sincere wish to make the most of them for our own sake as well as for others, it gains tremendous value. Think how you already have this human life that is valuable beyond compare. That in itself is sufficient for us to feel that we have something special and worthy of profound satisfaction. If we use this human life to develop our understanding of interdependence, it can make our human life of endless value for ourselves and others.

Life itself presents us with endless opportunities to deepen our awareness of the workings of interdependence and to reorient our daily interactions and experiences accordingly.

We do not actually need a book to learn about interdependence. Interdependence is happening all around us all the time. It is pervasive. We can easily educate ourselves by simply observing our own experience. Everything we do and sense can become a reminder of the value of interdependence.

When we sip our tea or coffee, start our car, enter a shop, or exchange greetings with someone while out for a stroll, we are enjoying those experiences as a direct result of interdependence. All these moments bear direct witness to the workings of interdependence. Such daily occurrences are a continuous procession of opportunities to recognize that others are indispensable to our well-being. They can inspire us continually to appreciate what others are contributing to our happiness, to feel grateful for them, and to treasure them.

We can use such moments to further our cultivation of humility, confidence, or any of the inner qualities we have determined to deepen. These moments can transform interdependence from an idea into something we feel and value highly. It is in the course of our everyday lives that we can awaken to the reality of our interdependence and begin to live according to this basic underlying principle. When we are fully experiencing interdependence—living it—it is no longer an idea. It has become a way of life—a principled way of life.

THE REFUGE OF LOVE

My own life provided me with experience in coming to terms with what it means to be an interdependent individual. From the time I was small, I was told I was the reincarnation of someone special and would have some important role to play. At the time of my birth, people had observed signs—the appearance of cuckoo birds, a sound like a conch shell resounding throughout the valley—that they considered to be indications that I was someone remarkable. For years they did not know who exactly, because no one had been able to recognize whose reincarnation I was.

For that reason I was able to live a fairly ordinary life with my family until, at the age of seven, I was recognized as the reincarnation of the Sixteenth Karmapa. Then, in a very short period of time, I was taken from my home, separated from my parents and playmates and all that had been familiar to me, brought to an unfamiliar place, and surrounded by people I did not know. Everything was completely new to me.

Looking at this one way, you could say I lost my personal freedom. It might seem to you that my human rights were violated, that I had lost the freedom to decide my own future, and was simply told now you have to be the Karmapa and do the job of a Karmapa. My case may seem extreme, but in different ways, we are all in this same position. We all face conditions in life that we did not choose. This, too, is part of interdependence. Some of the conditions that affect our lives are ones we have chosen and others we would have gladly avoided. Some such conditions are within us and others are outside us. Part of the task of learning to live as interdependent individuals is to find ways to make this productive for us.

When I was first named Karmapa, I imagined that being the Karmapa would mean I'd get more toys and have more playmates and more games to play. Was I wrong! It swiftly became clear that being the Karmapa entailed huge responsibilities and required me to engage in extensive studies.

In order to properly fulfill those responsibilities, I left Tibet and came to India when I was fourteen. Since I arrived in India, I have had many new opportunities, and there has been much benefit in my being here. Yet I still face many challenges stemming from my position as a spiritual leader in Tibetan Buddhism. For example, I cannot just go wherever I wish but must apply for formal travel permission well in advance of going anywhere. This naturally becomes an obstacle for me to be able to fulfill the responsibilities I have as the Karmapa.

As a result, I have had to greatly reduce my expectations of what I will be able to accomplish. I have had to cultivate a feeling of satisfaction with whatever little I can do. I reflect that I am still alive, and I am living this life primarily cherishing and supporting others, trying to serve as a sort of refuge where others can be assured of finding love.

This is the value I hold most dear and what has given meaning to my life. In the future as well, even if I cannot benefit them in any substantial way, if I live my life holding in my heart affection and concern for others, then at least I can offer them the knowledge that they have someone who cares deeply for them. Even if I can do nothing more for them at the moment, I tell myself as long as I am alive, I will offer my support and love to them.

All those connected to me will be able to take comfort in the knowledge that they have at least one person in the world who sincerely and completely cares about them. Knowing that my presence is providing them with just this small condition of comfort and ease gives me a sense of meaning and purpose to my life, limited though I am in opportunities to be of practical help to others. Even if I do not have the ideal external conditions to work toward my aims, I am sustained by the awareness that others are dependent on me and have placed their hopes in me. For me, the basic fact of my interdependence is a source of courage and determination.

Once we fully embrace our connections to others, we can intentionally breathe life into them, and this can fill our lives with meaning and love.

FOUR

Equality and Diversity

WE ARE LIVING IN a historical moment when there is great awareness of human diversity as well as a much broader commitment to the ideal of human equality than we have had in the past. The notion of full equality is being extended across many social categories that were historically used to divide societies, such as race, religion, and sex or gender. Advocates for justice in various arenas continue to work toward an unbounded ideal of equality that is even more encompassing, to include others who in the recent past, or still today, have been labeled as unequal, impaired, or even unnatural, on account of their sexual orientation or gender identity or other physical or mental conditions.

To nurture this positive development, it is paramount that we get clear and keep in focus the actual foundation of our equality. We need a clear understanding of what makes us equal, so that when we encounter the inevitable diversity that arises as we are impacted by diverse causes and conditions, we do not mistake these differences as an indication of inequality. By virtue of having a mind or awareness, all sentient beings are equal in terms of our capacity to experience pain and joy, in our pervasive longing to avoid suffering and to be happy. This deeply held wish is the basis of our equality and is far more fundamental than our differences. It lies at the heart of all our aspirations and actions.

What's more, all human beings are equal in our capacity to cultivate the inner conditions on which our happiness depends, as individuals and also as a society: empathy, love, and a courageous compassion. These premises—our desire to be happy and our shared inner potential to create the conditions that lead to happiness—form the foundation of universal human equality.

We are also equal in depending on the earth to sustain us. We may occupy different places on the globe and our lives may be affected by local conditions, but we all share this planet and all breathe its air. Because of interdependence, actions in one part of the world affect other parts. A market demand for a particular good in one corner of the globe may have led to excessive carbon emissions by factories in another corner where that item is produced. The skies could be clear and healthy where you buy the product, while the air breathed by the factory workers and their families may be full of smog, and it could be rare to even see blue skies. Differences emerge in terms of the conditions we live in, but we all equally need clean air and long to see the deep blue sky above us; all parents are equally distressed if their children fall ill with breathing ailments. Therefore, although we are equal, clearly equality is not sameness. Interdependence shows us that we cannot be identical, because we cannot occupy an identical place in the chain of causes and conditions that connect us all. However, from whatever diverse place we occupy in our interdependent world, we all deserve equal access to our shared resources.

In Tibetan, we speak of sameness and difference in terms of roots and branches, and would say that individuals and societies differ in terms of the branches but not in terms of the root. Since at our deepest level, the level of our roots, we are equal, I see no real need for us to be the same in all the subsidiary aspects. In fact, the diversity that is found on the level of our branches is actually beneficial and wholesome for our interdependent world and for all of us individually.

As we live our lives as equals within interdependence, we manifest different cultural assumptions and different religious views or philosophies of life. This diversity greatly enhances the richness of human culture that we can all learn and benefit from. We differ in terms of our lifestyles, our opinions, our gender identities, our racial characteristics, our bodies, and in countless other ways. These differences do not undermine or subtract from our human equality; they do not make us more or less human.

THE MARKETING OF "EQUALITY"

Despite the broad intellectual acceptance of the ideal of equality, we generally do not feel equal, and we certainly do not act like we are all equal. There remains both a great deal of actual social inequality and a great deal of perceived personal inequality.

Globalization and consumerism encourage everyone to aspire equally to the same ideal of material prosperity. These two forces can have the effect of obscuring our real basis of equality, which is internal, as they maneuver us into chasing an illusory version of external equality based on material goods. Sometimes I feel that our consumer culture actually uses the ideal of equality as a marketing tool, to stimulate a personal sense of inequality that we can overcome only by buying more goods. Our global consumer culture has taught us to define ourselves in terms of our possessions and our purchasing power. We come to feel that being equal means adopting a similar lifestyle—a lifestyle that is largely constructed by corporations and promoted all over the world through social media. The global economy is fueled by the message that we are inadequate and incomplete as we are and we therefore need to acquire things to make up for that lack. The message is this: If you do not stay up to date with the latest trends in fashion and the latest version of personal electronics, you cannot consider yourself equal to those who do.

Given the never-ending procession of goods still out there waiting to be purchased, we are practically guaranteed to feel that we fall short of the mark. We are constantly measuring ourselves against others and ranking ourselves in terms of having more or less. Those who have all the trappings of consumer success simply come to seem more equal than others, and those who do not have the best brands seem substandard. This deceptive standard of equality feeds a self-perpetuating cycle of consumption. It makes us feel that we should be equal but have failed.

This is because we are not sufficiently clear about what truly makes us equal to others. As a result, we end up believing that we are truly equal only when we have the same stuff. Not knowing the basis of our true worth leaves us terribly impoverished. It also constitutes a serious obstacle in our efforts to establish a reliable basis for social equality.

WHAT IS DEVELOPMENT, REALLY?

The same dynamic operates on the level of entire communities. Any community or demographic group that has not reached the forefront of the scramble to consume is dubbed "backward" and one whose voice can therefore be ignored in conversations about global issues. They are seen as still in need of "development." This reflects an unthinking embrace of modernity's so-called progress.

Not long ago, a few Amazonian communities were contacted who it seems had previously had no contact with the outside world. Up until this century they had managed to preserve their sustainable way of living in the rainforest. Learning of this, people marveled at their exotic way of life and picturesque customs. But at the same time, they imagined these Amazon communities as backward and primitive, living like that without any modern conveniences. The nomadic community that I grew up in as a small boy was different in that we did have some contact with other cultures, but as I mentioned, we also managed without electricity, appliances, or even anything made of plastics. We nomads were similarly looked down on as backward and considered by many to be in dire need of development.

The challenge of developing wisely raises some serious issues. To start with, what do we mean by development? We need to differentiate much more carefully between wise development and mere material advancement. In many areas, the understanding of development has been broadened to include such goals as human rights, environmental conservation, and education. Yet all too often, people still believe they are witnessing "development" when they see "backward" sectors finding new opportunities to do menial jobs for low pay, so that they can buy more of the consumer goods that are the markers of success and advancement.

We can develop as human beings in many different ways. Not all are aimed at giving more access to consumer goods. Development could also bring better access to other conditions for happiness and well-being. More value could be placed on development of inner conditions for growth as a human being.

However we develop, we should do so in such a way that everyone has equal access to beneficial advancements and resources. We must also consider what that access costs not only financially, but also in terms of a community's cultural identity and therefore of human diversity as a whole. Now that we have encountered the Amazon communities, should we leave them alone to pursue their own way of life, or should they receive educational and other resources comparable to what the rest of the world has access to? There is no easy answer. If we give them a modern education, they will inevitably begin to lose many of the forms of knowledge that preserve their own way of life and that they have upheld for thousands of years. Yet if women are dying in childbirth, or if other members of the community are suffering from diseases we have the cure to, surely we should offer them access to medical treatment and the education that will lead them to prevent such diseases.

Many forms of traditional local knowledge and sustainable local practices are being replaced by the products of multinational corporations. The Amazonian communities surely hold invaluable knowledge about the resources preserved in the unequaled biodiversity of that region. In the case of the Tibetan plateau, we had a way of life that respected a fragile ecosystem that urgently needs to be kept healthy, because it is the source of Asia's major rivers and of so much frozen freshwater that it is known as the world's Third Pole. The whole world stands to lose when such local ways of life and the knowledge they transmit are lost.

I want to make clear that I am not arguing categorically against change when it could improve health and well-being. Like everyone else in the world, I very much want my family members to have access to healthcare when they are sick. My point is that these are complex issues that need thoughtful, studied consideration. One consideration should be the costs to the survival of traditional, local practices that the whole world benefits from. There should be global conversations, and space should be made for the voices of those who do not exemplify the global ideals of material development.

There is no doubt that we are all equals on a fundamental human level, but we need to think further about how we are managing our obvious differences. How can we establish social equality without erasing diversity? How can we embrace our differences with mutual respect and harmony?

DIFFERENCE IS NOT DEFICIENCY

To begin to explore such questions, we need to address several points of confusion. We seem to have a great deal of difficulty distinguishing between being equal and being the same. When we reduce the ideal of human equality to an idea of sameness, great harm results at every level of reality. This is especially true when the ideal we are all encouraged to aspire to has been determined by the self-interests of a few.

The beauty industry is a clear example of this. Consciously or unconsciously, many people have come to yearn to have the same facial features and body shape that they have seen in a magazine or other media. They may go to great lengths to match such images of outer beauty. Women are particularly encouraged to feel they must wear cosmetics and "make over" their face and bodies. We can see sexism at work in this message that having a physical appearance that pleases others is key to a woman's success in life.

Many people do not stop at applying creams or going to the gym, but actually submit voluntarily to surgical procedures in this quest to meet physical standards that have been set by others. Believe it or not, I even saw a video that compared the big eyes I had as a young boy to how I look nowadays, arguing that I must certainly have undergone plastic surgery to look more like the previous Karmapa. I had never even heard of the concept of plastic surgery before I arrived in India, so it all came as quite a shock to hear of such a thing. But it shows how normal it seems to people to alter their bodies so they match up to some image—they imagine even a Buddhist monk would do so!

All around the world—not only in the materially developed countries but anywhere people have disposable cash—there are doctors who cater to this wish. Korean friends of mine tell me that South Korea is known for having particularly skillful cosmetic surgeons. Apparently numerous Korean women have shown their surgeon the photo of the woman considered to be the most beautiful—the winner of the Miss Korea beauty pageant—and asked to be made to look like her. As a result, now there are ten or twenty women in Korea who are all difficult to tell apart, or so I have been told.

Whether or not this actually happened, the existence of a billion-dollar industry that both stimulates and profits from our longing to look like someone else is deeply, deeply troubling. The idea that there could be a single ideal face of beauty is not only ridiculous but terribly harmful. Why on earth do we think we all need to look the same?

This is a sign we have confused difference with deficiency. When that happens, equality gets translated into uniformity and sameness. We can see this happening in our thirst to meet external standards of beauty and success. We assess whether we are doing well by comparing ourselves to others and seek to have what others have, to act like others, and even to look like others.

Our idea of equality must go deeper. Our equality is based not in what we have or how we look, but in who we are. We are equal in our shared human condition and in the latent nobility of heart that lies within each of us. When we make that the standard of our equality and our value, we all already measure up. We can find the basis for living as equals without needing to reduce equality to conformity.

THE VALUE OF DIVERSITY

Just as the view of interdependence teaches us to value biodiversity in the natural environment, the view of interdependence can help us value human diversity. Interdependence can lead us to appreciate the benefits—and the beauty—of our differences.

Although we share the same inner potential for goodness and longing for happiness, we human beings are born into different contexts, and we develop different interests, habits, and inclinations. On a personal level, we each differ due to our individual interactions and experiences, and human societies also display great cultural diversity due to their distinct histories and contexts. This human diversity contributes to the strength and health of our societies, just as plant diversity contributes to the strength and health of a forest.

One area where we seem to find it particularly difficult to accept our differences—much less value them—is religion. However, religious diversity is inevitable, given the diversity in the historical and cultural conditions that give rise to religious institutions, doctrines, and practices. What's more, religious diversity is also necessary and positive for human society. Since human beings are diverse in terms of our predispositions and needs, we benefit greatly from having a variety of spiritual paths available to us. From a Buddhist perspective, the argument that one religion is the best while the rest are all mistaken or inferior is unsustainable and not useful. It fails to take into account our variety of human dispositions and emotional needs. If it does not suit our individual temperament or help us to free ourselves from suffering and become better people, following the "best" religion is of little use. Even if one religion were really the best or truest, I do not think that being the best and truest is the point when it comes to religion. In my view, the point is for it to suit the person and to benefit them.

There is no reason to insist that everyone follow a single religion or spiritual path, or for all religions to agree on the same beliefs and practices in order to be considered equal. In fact, religions are already equal in the most important sense. If they address us as human beings, recognizing our common wish to be free of suffering and to find lasting happiness, they are equal. They are united in a common goal, which is to alleviate suffering and help us find happiness and live meaningful lives. All religions offer us ways to achieve these aims by looking primarily within our own hearts and minds. I think when we recognize this shared purpose at the root of all religions, we will be able to see them as fundamentally equal and to respect and value the diversity we see in their branches—their particular forms and expressions.

The twenty-first century is a century of sharing. The fact that we are engaged in constant exchanges is an integral effect of the communications age. Nearly everywhere we go the world is so thoroughly penetrated by wireless signals that we are constantly exposed to others. By the same token, we have access to images, information, and ideas from all corners of our globe. Our world today offers a historically unprecedented freedom to interact across cultural and religious borders. It remains to be seen precisely *how* our sharing will manifest as the twenty-first century continues and how that sharing will change us. As we will explore in chapter 9, on sharing global resources, we may not be very skilled at it yet, but sharing, of one form or another, is here to stay.

As interdependence shows us, whenever there is contact, both parties are impacted and changed in some way or another, subtle or obvious. World history records a remarkable diversity of cultures, views, and religions, and encounters between them have had a wide range of consequences, negative as well as positive.

Some communities have adapted and intermingled with others, some set out to dominate other communities, while others actively sought to preserve and defend their way of life and their views within their own bounded territories. In past centuries, when communication was slower and movement across borders was more complicated, communities and countries were able to retain a greater degree of distinctness than is possible today. Even within the impenetrable rainforests of the Amazon, much less anywhere else on the face of a planet as wired as ours, there is no place one can go to escape contact with the rest of the world.

Today our diversity is something to be shared and exchanged with others freely. Each culture and religion is no longer the property of any single community but is available to all who live on this planet to learn from. This is simply a feature of the twenty-first-century world we live in, and it is time we recognize this and adopt the attitudes appropriate to this shift in our way of sharing the world. This means learning to truly value one another and to recognize diversity as highly productive and beneficial. Previously, due to limitations in our education and outlook, we automatically privileged our own views and unthinkingly deemed others' as inferior. This sort of judgmental approach has no rightful place in a century of sharing.

The globalization of consumer culture poses a further danger. When we encounter the knowledge and practices of other cultures online or in other circumstances where they have been disconnected from their living human context, it may seem as if they belong to no one and that we can therefore do with them what we wish. We may even feel that we are showing appreciation by doing so. But religious traditions and cultural practices are not yet another set of products to be acquired and consumed. That is a kind of spiritual materialism or cultural appropriation and not genuine human sharing.

Ideally, sharing across differences entails a genuine openness on our part to learn *from* other traditions, and not just learn about them or consume the parts of them we like. It can require us to move out from behind our computers and truly connect with the people whose wisdom and traditions we wish to learn from. In order for such encounters to be meaningful, they must challenge us on some level. This requires that we listen attentively to other traditions, taking care not to project our own meanings and assumptions on what they are telling us. If we do so, as we engage with new ideas and new practices, ultimately they will change us and allow us to discover new possibilities for living as humans on this planet. Authentic sharing means being open to the possibility that the other will change you.

At a minimum, a century of sharing requires that we value others' worldviews. If we feel we cannot sincerely value a particular culture or religion for itself, then at least we should be willing to recognize its purpose and its reason for being, and respect and appreciate its existence in the world on that basis. To do so, we need to recognize the tremendous value in having such diversity available to us in the world. Our valuing of diversity is grounded in the more fundamental level of common sense and common values, and of common human needs and aspirations.

That is to say, our valuing of diversity is grounded in an awareness of our basic equality. This recognition gives us a solid basis for not just tolerating or accepting our differences but actually cherishing them. It also lets us see that difference is in no way a threat to equality. Rather, our equality makes the presence of diversity of such great value. Our differences are comparatively superficial relative to the shared roots of human equality, and our differences in fact are necessary.

THE CONSEQUENCES OF IGNORANCE

All too often we respond to difference in a way that is very far from this vision of sharing. Rather than encountering the other on our fundamental shared ground and approaching them there with a wish to truly understand and come closer, much of the time we react out of ignorance.

Into the vacuum created by our basic ignorance about others, we heap our own projections. We take isolated details and flesh them out into full-blown fictions, or we uncritically adopt them from the media or society. When we do not recognize or acknowledge our own ignorance about others, we believe in these fictions. If we apply the value of humility that we discussed in chapter 3, we can recognize that we do not have full knowledge of who the other person is. This helps us stay open to learning about them. We do not make the mistake of thinking we already know all that we need to know about them when in fact we know next to nothing.

If we analyze our perceptions of others carefully, we can see that we fall into various subtle forms of ignorance. Often we see one aspect of a person and think we have seen them in their totality. We take a part and think it is the whole. This is ignorance. People who create beautiful art may have ethical behavior that we would find repugnant, and a person we observe lashing out in a moment of hurt may be far gentler than us most of the time.

What's more, we also ascribe a false reality to something that has merely been imputed. This is a bit more subtle. Let's take a person's name. Tibetan names are hard for non-Tibetans, so I usually use the name Jack as an example. The person who bears the name Jack was not born with that name emblazoned on his newborn body. Yet once this tag was assigned to him, he believes that he is Jack. In actual fact, he is not naturally or inherently Jack. It was just applied to him as a convention. But later, since he thinks he is really Jack, he feels pain or delight based on how people speak of Jack. If the letters of the word Jack disperse, there is nothing left. But he clings to those letters as if his life depended on them. People say something harsh about Jack, and he feels hurt and angry. His name is just a collection of letters, a mere designation. It is not the actual person. Nevertheless, he acts as if he must live up to the labels that have been placed on him.

We all do this. On the one hand, we have names that we use, identities that we ascribe to ourselves and others, and the ideas we have about things. On the other hand, we have the things themselves. We constantly fail to distinguish between the two. We fail to recognize when we are operating on the level of words and labels and not the actual people or things themselves. We exercise our intellect to manipulate concepts and think that we are actually connecting with reality. This may look like a display of intelligence, but it is actually ignorance.

Ignorance denies our own role in producing the ideas that we have about others. Ignorance ignores the many interconnections that link us to others and the way those interconnections shape our views of one another. Ignorance's field of vision is partial, as it isolates people and things and treats them as truly separable from the cultural and personal contexts that form part of who and what they are. It imputes characteristics that we have conceptualized—or exaggerates some aspect that interests us—and leads us to think we are simply observing reality as it is. We focus on fictions we ourselves have written and think we are reading the truth.

This conflation of our ideas with actual reality is not just a matter of ignorance, but becomes especially dangerous when we take one idea and apply it to a whole class of people. Or we see one person and take them to represent a whole ethnic group or nationality. People hold so strongly onto the ideas they have that they continue to take them for reality even in the face of evidence to the contrary.

In Tibet, people from my part of the country are known as Khampas, and Khampas are believed to be aggressive and prone to fighting. People think that all Khampas are warlike and brave, and feel fear at the thought of confrontation with them. But I am a Khampa, and if you pick a fight with me, you will just see my back as I run away from you! I don't want to fight anyone.

Along with creating walls among people, this kind of ignorance easily gives rise to fear. Fear becomes a self-perpetuating mechanism for bigotry that is readily manipulated and can seep into many aspects of our lives. Since September 11th in the United States and elsewhere, when people see a Muslim they imagine they are looking at a member of Al Qaeda or ISIS. After the Boston Marathon bombing in 2013, the suspicion was aimed not only at people from the Middle East but at anyone who came from overseas to study in the United States. Then after the tragic terrorist attacks in Paris and California in 2015, and Brussels in 2016, the fear and distrust was redirected toward migrants to Europe or America who were seeking shelter from war and its aftermath. The actions of a handful of people shape how we label millions of people whose wish for happiness is equal to our own.

In America, there is great value placed on personal liberty and the right to dress as one pleases. Yet when some groups exercise that liberty by wearing clothes that reflect a cultural or religious tradition, even those who consider themselves liberal and open-minded close their minds in the face of such differences. They take one look and brand the others as closed-minded conservatives or even fanatics.

People who are considered the dominant or most powerful group in a society can put on business suits or some other standard form of dress, and then those who diverge from this norm are subtly judged to be outsiders or less equal. I think it is worth asking who gets to set the standards that others must emulate in order to fit in. Is it the majority or it is an elite? And why are the rest of us so determined to appear like them?

If we analyze this confusion whereby we take projections and appearances to be reality, and we ask ourselves how we became so caught up in labels and identities, we can trace the problem back to a basic problem of selfishness. We cling to our judgments and impressions simply because they are our own. This is a form of arrogance. We feel that what appears to us must be reality and what appears to others, if it is different, must be mistaken. Underneath this, our self-centered biases and myopic and distorted perspectives are busy at work filtering appearances and selecting what we notice and take as important. Humility can help us recognize that appearances show us only a part of what we need to see. Rather than simply taking our limited views as the truth, we could ask how things appear to others. There is great value in seeing through the eyes of others as well as our own.

HIERARCHY AND POWER

In today's global society, the dynamics of equality and difference play out in complex ways. We seem to take differences in our circumstances as a sign that we are somehow inherently different. This happens whenever equality is measured primarily through external measures. We make those differences a matter of better or worse, and create social hierarchies that we believe are natural and fixed and not a matter of social construction. From the perspective of interdependence, however, such hierarchies can be seen to be neither inherent nor permanent.

Hierarchies are a place we can see clearly the play of interdependence, and especially the aspect of mutual interdependence. Those at the top depend on those below just as much as vice versa. Often we assume that the powerless are inherently more dependent than the powerful. But this is not the case. Their dependence is just more visible and more readily recognized as dependency.

The famous and powerful are completely dependent on others both for their fame and their power. Fame depends on other people, who are your public. Announcing your accomplishments in an uninhabited place will not bring you renown. At best, shouting your own praises in an empty valley might make you a bit crazy! It cannot make you famous, if there are no witnesses. Being a powerful person implies power over others, so without people over whom to exercise your power, you cannot have the kind of power that puts you in privileged positions in a hierarchy. Leaders need followers, every bit as much as followers need leaders.

Whoever you are, and whatever your place in society, your happiness and well-being depend on others. Others' happiness similarly depends on you, naturally, as a matter of course. If everyone around you falls into hard times, you will also be affected eventually. Conversely, if they are flourishing and happy, this will certainly have some positive impact on your situation. It is for this simple reason that a concern for others, an altruistic orientation, is appropriate and in fact necessary. If this attitude is present, even if the relations between people are hierarchical, those people will help one another.

Those who have been given a certain power over others through hierarchical relationships are neither inherently superior nor inferior to anyone else. What makes us equal is not the place we occupy in a social order but the fact that we are human beings and therefore endowed with the potential for goodness and the capacity to feel pain and joy. Hierarchy is just a provisional way of ordering people in society, bringing them into relationships where each is giving and receiving something from others.

There are many types of hierarchies, but none are permanent or eternally ordained. Rather, each has come about for specific purposes and to achieve specific aims. For example, governments are organized hierarchically, and a great deal of power might be concentrated in the hands of a president or prime minister, and this is done with the aim of benefiting the country or its people.

Sometimes people fail to appreciate this fact, and mistake a privileged place in a hierarchy as an opportunity to further their personal interests. This is an abuse of the hierarchy and is ultimately counterproductive. It goes against the very reason for organizing ourselves in that hierarchy in the first place. If a person is not able or willing to fulfill the function for which they are occupying that place in the hierarchy, sooner or later they will be removed from it. However, in the meantime, a great deal of damage can be done.

This is why it is so important for people at all levels of society to understand the interdependent nature of relationships in hierarchies and to be taught a sense of universal responsibility and a basic concern for others. It is also important to be aware that hierarchies are social orders we create ourselves for particular purposes in particular historical conditions. When a hierarchy has outlasted its purpose, it is time to look for other ways to organize ourselves.

No matter how clearly we recognize that we are naturally equal, there remains a great deal of inequality in the world. These inequities are not natural but are almost all entirely man-made.

What is the basis for our society today? What determines who gains access to the means of pursuing their happiness and well-being? It seems this is not based on the yearning we each have for happiness—which is equal in all of us. Rather it seems to be based on who has power and who has access to power through wealth. Access to education is a crucial condition as well. Our education helps determine our economic opportunities, and money is made a condition for access to healthcare and to other means of eliminating our suffering and securing happiness. No wonder there is so much inequality. Do we not all have an equal right to happiness?

When we encounter social inequalities, we tend to want to point the finger and find someone to blame. But no one else has created these inequities and left us this mess. We human beings have made this mess of inequity, collectively, and likewise we are responsible for cleaning it up.

Most often we feel it is primarily the fault of those running the government, the policy makers, the CEOs of the multinational corporations, or whoever is at the top of our power hierarchies. But this is a false argument. As we have just discussed, those who are identified as the power makers are in those positions because of those below them in the hierarchy. If we fail to vote against them, if we silently go along with their policies, if we buy their products and support their business practices, we are forming an ongoing part of their power base. We all have a responsibility—and a part to play in this interdependent world—to ensure that all have access to what they need to alleviate suffering.

The single biggest issue we are facing this century is the environmental crisis. This, too, is the manifestation of a failure to honor basic equality—not only the equality within human society, but with other species and with the planet itself. This planet is the common home of all the species who inhabit it. Yet in the 100,000 years or so since we Homo sapiens walked off the savannah, we have grabbed the reins and insisted on steering things on this planet.

We have taken over by force, inflicting terrible pain and damage on everything and everyone in our way. The number of animals we have killed for our own comfort, pleasure, or entertainment is inconceivable. We have caused them unthinkable pain and agony, although animals have as intense a wish to escape pain and suffering as we do. This is one huge instance of inequity. Since we champion such inequality on this interspecies and planetary level, it is not surprising that we human beings do the same to one another.

Setting aside what we have done to other species, take, for example, how we divide ourselves based on differences in sex and gender. We create entire identities based on these categories and then see ourselves as inherently and fundamentally different from people who identify themselves differently.

Certainly we can find biological differences, but just look at how these have been made into social differences. Not only do we feel that men and women have entirely different natures, but we also create power hierarchies based on those differences. We might concede that, in the distant past, there was some aim accomplished by giving men some more social power. In the initial stages of our evolution as humans, the sort of physical strength that is more common to men than to women could be a key factor in the survival of the species or clan. In waging war and hunting large prey, muscle power did give a great advantage.

But times have changed. Just looking at the technology we have available to us today, it is obvious that it is not brute force we most need. It is mental power. Most urgently needed today are inner qualities such as empathy, openness, caring, and gentleness. If we are going to assign a gender to the qualities we most need, it is more likely to be feminine than masculine.

As I mentioned, when the historical need that gave rise to a hierarchy changes, there is no basis for clinging to that hierarchy. However, when those whom this hierarchy benefits use their power to preserve their advantage and ensure that they remain on top, it takes concerted effort to change, on the part of men as well as women.

When some men hear the term *women's rights*, they feel threatened, as if a competition for rights was being announced, and they are in danger of losing some of their rights and having to hand them over to women. They think it is like a divorce where the property has to be divided up between the husband and the wife, or children feuding over who inherits what from the parents. If the other person receives something, you feel it is at your cost.

This is a misunderstanding of what human rights are. I think it would be more productive to think first in terms of basic worth. We recognize others' worth and therefore seek to ensure they have the rights they truly deserve as human beings.

In the end, our efforts to extend equal rights to all in our global society will succeed or fail based on whether or not we can connect with the real ground of our equality. When we lose sight of that common ground, our differences are all too often treated as matters of higher or lower. When this happens, diversity looks like an obstacle to real equality.

Interdependence offers a way to see instead the great value in diversity and to recognize that equality does not require uniformity. But in order for our equality to be a value we live by, and not an abstract principle we are willing to endorse only verbally, we also need to learn new habits of connecting from the heart across differences. To that end, our basic capacity for empathy is a powerful resource we can develop to connect on that deeper level.

FEELING THE CONNECTION

FIVE

From Empathy to Courageous Compassion

W E HAVE MANY POSITIVE qualities within us—qualities like empathy, courage, and wisdom. We might call these qualities the values of interdependence. These values are among the many conditions within us that interact among themselves and with outer conditions to shape our lives and our world. Actively cultivating these qualities helps us go beyond a theoretical understanding of interdependence, to begin actually feeling ourselves to be profoundly interconnected. As we increase our emotional awareness of interdependence, our whole inner world changes in profound ways, and these changes have profound implications for how we relate to the world around us.

Sometimes when we speak of an inner world, it might sound like a place separate from the world around us, somewhere we can escape to where no one and nothing can reach us. Everything we have seen of interdependence should make it clear that there is no such place. There are no worlds that are apart from all other worlds.

Our inner world evolves in conjunction with our outer world. It shapes our interpretations and emotional responses to what we see around us, suggests possible courses of action based on those interpretations and our own aims, and produces the intentions to carry them out. This in turn changes our external circumstances, and from there the cycles of mutual impact continue.

We are generally much more aware of the impact our outer circumstances have on our inner states and tend to grossly underestimate the effect of our inner world on the outer world. The world inside our hearts and minds is made of different "material" than the physical world. Perceptions, emotions, thoughts, and intentions form part of the composition of our inner world, and so do all our other affective and cognitive capacities. These capacities are not physical, but they have the power to reshape the world.

We hold within us the power of compassion and wisdom, the power of discernment and intentional action, the powers of imagination and human intelligence, and even of skill in using technology. They work interdependently within us to allow us to experience true freedom, inspire us to take up our responsibility, and greatly extend the scope of our impact on the world.

In the following chapters, we will be exploring these values and various other inner forces to gain greater emotional as well as intellectual understanding of how our inner conditions work together. This allows us to strengthen those that favor happiness and reduce those that provoke dissatisfaction and suffering—for ourselves and others.

WALKING A MILE TOWARD A COMMON GOAL

Empathy plays a powerful role in moving the awareness of interdependence from our heads to our hearts and from there into compassionate action. The interconnections that link us to others are not solely physical. We are profoundly connected emotionally to others as well, and our capacity for empathy is a palpable sign of that emotional connectedness.

Although we are in fact profoundly interconnected and interdependent, the dominant concept of ourselves as independent individuals encourages us to see ourselves as separate and fundamentally disconnected. Through empathy, we can not only know but actually feel that this view is distorted. By empathizing with others, we gain an emotional awareness of their inner experience, and in the process, we actually perceive our emotional connectedness. In this way, empathy reveals on an affective level what ignorance and egocentrism deny.

Empathy enables us to reach across differences and connect as equals. It does so by cutting straight through the walls that we build up around us and allowing us to touch the core of our equality: the ability to experience pain and joy.

More than just our own personal happiness and wisdom is at stake. In order to sustain the long-term action needed to cure the social inequities we have created in the world today, we need to be able to root ourselves firmly in the common ground of our equality as sentient beings. Empathy takes us along a direct route to that ground. It lets us actually *feel* what equality has told us to be true: that we are all equal in terms of our search for happiness and to avoid suffering, even as the particulars of our experience vary at any given moment.

This function of empathy is captured by an expression from the indigenous peoples of the Americas that speaks of walking a mile in another person's shoes. When we look at others or think of others, we can remind ourselves of our universal base of inner equality and then try to experience their situations from their perspective rather than our own. We are all trying to make our way forward as best we can toward our goal of happiness. Walking in another person's shoes allows us to feel their particular conditions and gain a sense for what moves them to take the route they did trying to reach the same ultimate goal that we seek. We stand inside their shoes and see their lives from the inside, not merely observing it from the outside.

On the basis of the empathy that arises when we connect in this way, we can see the specifics of a person's circumstances not as signs they are inherently different or other but as a manifestation of the same basic wish that we share with them.

CONNECTED RIGHT FROM BIRTH

Empathy allows us to become aware of others' situations and problems on an emotional level. There have been important debates for quite some time about whether human beings are naturally empathetic. Previously many people believed that empathy was not natural to us but rather was a product of nurture. However, more recently, studies of interaction among infants and very small children have shown that humans respond empathetically to others' suffering from the very start of our lives.

We can draw on ample observations in our own experience that also suggest that empathy is a natural human response. We wince when we see others injured. When others around us are rolling with laughter, we can find ourselves smiling even if we did not hear the joke. We have surely all experienced this and many other such instances that indicate an inherent ability to sense and share in others' feelings.

This ability to connect with the inner condition of others does not appear to be something humans need to be taught. You may have noticed that when one infant cries, others who hear their sounds of distress start crying as well. Babies are apparently moved by others' pain even before they learn to speak. When they grow a bit older and can walk, when one child is in tears, others will come over to him or her and hand them toys or hug and caress them in an effort to soothe them.

Neuroscientists have studied the reactions of small children watching another child slam his hand in a door, and their investigations showed that the pain matrices fired in the young brains when they simply saw the other child injured and crying. This and other research indicates that there is a neurological basis for the affective experience of empathy, present right from the beginning of our lives. In this sense, empathy can be thought of as hard-wired into our brains.

Of course, this does not mean that our empathy could never be weakened or even damaged. Although we are born with this inner quality of empathy, it can become less accessible to us over time. Indeed, nurture often seems actually to be diminishing our natural capacity.

Neuroscientists have also identified cases of people whose neural empathetic response is significantly weaker than the average. It does not appear that such people have no capacity for empathy whatsoever but rather that this area of their cerebral functioning is greatly reduced. Thus far, researchers have found no way to remedy this impairment surgically or medically.

But it is far more common—and of greater concern—that our empathy becomes impaired in the normal course of our upbringing. I believe it is time we asked ourselves collectively what we are doing in the socialization process that ends up diminishing the empathetic responses we observe so much more readily in children than in adults.

NO SOCIAL HEALTH WITHOUT IT

We invest immense resources in research for cures for illnesses such as cancer and heart disease. I think we can consider a lack of empathy to be a kind of disease as well. The apathetic response to the pain of others is a condition that has devastating consequences not only for those who suffer from it themselves but for everyone they encounter—in fact, for all of society. There can be no social health unless empathy is made a central value.

Normally people say malaria and dysentery are major world killers, but I think apathy kills more than any other single disease. We turn our backs on many people in pain, rather than extending a hand or offering a word of comfort, out of a failure to empathize. Because we feel indifferent to others' suffering, we walk away from many situations that we could have helped to change. On a broader societal level, many situations of violence, oppression, and sheer neglect are allowed to continue because our empathy is underdeveloped or even switched off.

Perhaps it would help to give a name to this condition, which we could call *empathy impairment*. This can draw our attention to the problems caused by our lack of empathy and could mobilize efforts to find ways to treat this dangerous condition.

In our interdependent age of connectivity, empathy must be a primary virtue. When we are constantly linked externally but cannot connect from the heart, remaining emotionally unaware of the experiences of others, we lose our basis to create a healthy global society. Given the extent of our connectedness, we need to care about the consequences of our words and actions on others. Empathy both keeps us concerned and helps us understand the experiences that our actions create in others. The engagement that empathy provides helps ensure that we make decisions with an awareness of the pain or delight that we might cause for others.

Empathy impairment is a particularly dangerous disease in leaders who are in a position to make a difference in social policy or practices. The US president Barack Obama has spoken of the urgent need for empathy in society, and points out how harmful it is to the entire country when its government is lacking in this essential quality. I think the public should make this one of the main qualifications that they require of any politician seeking their vote.

Actually, since there are scientific means to measure empathetic responses neurologically, I have a proposal. I am half joking of course, but imagine if, before a country holds political elections, candidates were required to undergo a neurological study to determine their level of empathy. They could be hooked up to the machines and see how they fare. If they failed the test, they could be required to undergo training until they came up to a certain mark, and only then be allowed to proceed with their election campaigns.

I realize this seems absurd, but imagine the impact it would have on the quality of life on this planet if we were to take empathy seriously as a qualification needed in order to be given the opportunity to lead the world. There are more realistic measures we could take toward that end. We could consciously review the records and speeches of those running for office, and actively assess how fully they display this central quality. Do they disregard or deny the feelings of others? Are they able to connect on a human basis with those who are different from them? Do they only engage with others who further their own political aims? Do they care about the consequences of their decisions on others? By asking such questions, we could make empathy a criterion for serving as a political leader.

HOW EMPATHY CAN BECOME IMPAIRED

Like all other aptitudes we are born with, empathy can be reinforced or weakened. We can intentionally provide better inner conditions for our own empathy to flourish. Alternatively we might end up nurturing destructive emotions and attitudes not favorable for empathy. Similarly, some external environments encourage the strengthening of empathy while others discourage it. Those politicians I just mentioned might have entered politics with their empathy functioning at healthy levels but ended up operating at reduced levels of empathy because they found it consistently blocked or attacked. This can happen to all of us. Although, as the studies show, we all start out with the capacity for empathy, if we live in environments where it is a distinct disadvantage to be sensitive and caring, the growth of our empathy and compassion can become stunted.

We can ask how our global society fares in this regard. People are constantly pitted against one another, as competition and greed are stimulated and celebrated. Our sense of ourselves as separate and independent is activated and reinforced in many ways. From school age onward, social dynamics are set up that encourage us to see ourselves in a race to be the one to win prizes and praise that cannot be shared. We come to feel that we must struggle through our lives as if it were a battle to prevail over others or prevent them from prevailing. This creates contexts in which not only is there no space for empathy; it is actively impeded. If we wish to nurture empathy as an important quality for creating a sustainable interdependent world, we may need to rethink many of our educational and social practices.

In the meantime, what do we do about empathy that has already been weakened? As a preliminary step, we recognize how much is lost when our empathy is diminished. This awareness will encourage us to devote serious attention to addressing this harmful condition. Our next step is to explore strategies for bringing our empathy up to full strength.

It is not a case of needing to start from absolute zero, since empathy is inherently present in all of us. Therefore our task is more a matter of developing something that has been underdeveloped, or restoring something that has become weak or restricted. As I have noted, our natural capacity for empathy seems to decline as we age. This may be because we simply were not given the conditions to build on our inherent ability to connect empathetically, or it may have been discouraged through our upbringing or experiences in life.

The tendency to emphasize our differences and to create increasingly solid divisions based on race, class, or other limiting categories can also work against empathy. This limits the range within which we apply our empathy, as we mentally shut down our connection to certain others who do not fall within our preferred group. We can take Hitler as an instance of someone whose empathy was profoundly restricted in scope. While he was obviously incapable of feeling any empathy whatsoever toward Jews and many other groups of people, nevertheless Hitler is known to have displayed great tenderness and empathy toward certain dogs. As such, it does not appear he was completely incapable of empathy but that its scope was terribly limited. The challenge would be to train such people to broaden or transfer the feelings of tenderness and care that they are able to feel toward certain people or animals to other beings as well. Actually, we could all benefit from such training.

This is where consciously training in compassion and loving-kindness could come in. I will discuss more about how we can consciously cultivate these qualities in the third section of this book, but we can note here that this training proceeds by first strengthening the existing basis of empathy or compassion that we already have, and then extending it outward so as to be increasingly inclusive and increasingly intense. Since this is a process of mental training that builds on whatever basis one already has, it is well suited for starting from where we are now, with our empathy less than fully developed. Actually, until the moment when we have an unbearable, unconditional response to the suffering of all beings without exception, our empathy has not yet reached the limits of how far it can grow.

OUR BACKSTAGE PASS

When analyzing social problems, we are well trained to identify social, economic, and physical factors that serve as conditions responsible for producing the dynamics we wish to change. But inner and outer conditions are continually interacting to shape our actions, and thus to shape the world. For that reason, we also need to consider the internal conditions that lead people to act and react in certain ways.

We know that we cannot make full sense of anything when we take it out of context. When it comes to people's actions, motivation is a key aspect of the context. Motivation arises from within and guides an external course of action. We must find ways to look beyond people's visible conduct and gain a sense of the inner states and emotions that motivate that conduct.

We place far too much weight on our limited impressions of others and so are much too quick to judge. We only ever see part of the picture, and generally not the most important part. If life were a movie, much of the time we would just be watching the closing moments of the movie. We would not have seen entire series of events that led to the final scene appearing before us. This is why having an open mind is so important. When our mind and heart are open, we can better listen to what our empathy tells us. This helps us understand what is going on inside others, motivating them to act as they do.

There is always an unseen background. Each person has within them an inner emotional world, a backstory and a backstage where things have been evolving and are decided long before they are revealed to the public. Things never simply burst forth for no reason and with no impelling force whatsoever. Empathy can serve as a backstage pass, giving us access to the reasons and the forces impelling others' actions.

When we truly reach out to understand, we nearly always find something understandable there. We see what was going on inside a person, leading them to act as they did. We may ultimately find that action inexcusable, but at least we will have understood what was driving it. If we are not prepared to accept a behavior, in ourselves or in others, then we should learn how to help change it. To that end, understanding is key, for we can only bring about lasting changes in behavior by recognizing and addressing the inner and outer conditions that lead to it.

IN THE MOST CHALLENGING CASES

As incomprehensible as his later actions may be, one of the Boston bombers had expressed on social media that he felt friendless. He did not fit in and felt socially isolated. If we are not aware of the emotional turmoil raging inside those around us, we have little hope of anticipating violent behavior, much less reaching out to the person in order to prevent it.

We hear of sociopaths who were so starved for affection in their childhood that they have become cruel and callous, apparently losing their ability to empathize. They are unable to recognize the pain their victims feel, and they inflict pain on others or even kill them. Such extreme cases push the boundaries of our empathy. They also raise the question of whether a person can ever recover their empathy once they have completely lost it and, if so, how.

Buddhist texts tell the story of a serial-killer-turned-Buddhist-monk named Angulimala. He was born to a wealthy family and as a young boy was kind and well behaved. When he was old enough, his family sent him to the home of a brahman to be educated. His teacher's wife took a fancy to him, and one day when the teacher was out, she made romantic overtures to Angulimala, who rebuffed her advances. She took his refusal very badly, and when her husband came home, she claimed that the young man had attempted to seduce her.

The teacher was infuriated but concealed his wrath and determined to find a way to destroy Angulimala completely. He decided to describe to him a method that would purportedly make Angulimala semi-divine and virtually omnipotent. This method required that he kill a thousand people within a certain period of time, chopping off their fingers and wearing them as a necklace. The teacher was a great authority in the eyes of his students, and due to his student's trust in him, he was able to convince Angulimala that this was true. As a result, Angulimala murdered one person, then another, and thus embarked on a killing spree that left 999 people dead.

He had difficulty finding his last victim, since everyone naturally fled and hid behind locked doors whenever he was known to be in the area. Although Angulimala's behavior had given people many reasons to fear him, the Buddha was able to look beyond those reasons and intentionally placed himself in Angulimala's path. When they met, the Buddha, rather than trying to counter Angulimala's murderous actions by force, challenged him to stop himself. What the Buddha recognized that others could not was that Angulimala had the potential to change. This is only possible when we see that there is more to people than their actions and connect on a level beyond their external conduct. After his encounter with the Buddha, Angulimala became a monk and eventually became a source of inspiration to many people.

Just looking at Angulimala's behavior, it would be easy to consider him a lost cause, or even a monster. Yet the Buddha was able to turn him around completely, even after he had descended into such depths of depravity. The point is that no person, no matter how egregious their conduct, is beyond the reach of our understanding if we are able to extend ourselves toward them. But we must learn to look beyond their words and deeds to see the inner conditions that led to them.

CONDEMN THE BEHAVIOR, NOT THE PERSON

Our attitude toward terrorists could provide another useful limit case for our empathy. The response to the death of Osama bin Ladin is a case in point. When I heard that bin Ladin had been killed, my response was rather neutral. Normally, when someone loses their human life, it provokes some sense of sadness and loss. But I was aware that bin Ladin was responsible for the deaths of many people, and as such his life had caused great suffering and harm to others. For this reason, I did not feel quite the way I most often do when I hear of someone's death. I simply thought, "Oh, I see. He is dead."

I was staying in a hotel in Delhi, and I saw on the news that huge crowds had gathered in the United States, outside the White House, to celebrate and shout victory slogans. Had the victory been won by affecting a change of heart in bin Ladin, there would be cause for rejoicing. Perhaps you might not mourn his death, but to dance and sing because a bullet managed to locate the enemy and end his life was going way too far, I felt.

I had the thought that by dancing like this at the death of one enemy, in that very moment they were giving birth to many new enemies. This is how cycles of hatred and harm are perpetuated, with both sides unable to see that the other has any reasonable basis for thinking and acting as they do. The belief that our enemies are utterly unlike us is a significant problem. It is a major part of how enemies are created in the first place—and it is a part that we ourselves can change.

We need to distinguish the person from their actions. We can condemn their behavior, but we should not dismiss the person. We should not judge the person as a whole by their behavior in any given moment but take into account all the factors affecting them over time. There is more to a person than just the particular action that we are witnessing and disliking. If we are willing to look, we can always find another aspect of them that we are able to connect to and work with.

Despite our efforts to bring terrorist activity to an end, it seems only to be increasing. The term *terrorists* is applied nowadays to all sorts of groups, and this becomes an excuse to spy on, attack, or imprison people, and otherwise limit their freedoms. Bombing their strong-holds or killing their leaders may temporarily disrupt the group's activities, but it does not reduce their hatred or inspire them to act with compassion and kindness. If we do not address the causes and conditions that give rise to terrorism but only seek to stop each new manifestation of it, we will never uproot terrorism. Killing terrorists will never end terrorism. I find it terribly sad that we see killing as a means to that end. The exact same can be said of any other socially destructive behavior. It can be changed by changing the conditions that gave rise to it, not by destroying those who engage in it.

Even as we seek to foil their plots, the longer-term challenge is to understand why people came to take such extreme positions in the first place. I realize that we may be faced with acts of such cruelty that we may feel no wish to comprehend them. But no one becomes a terrorist by accident or for no reason; nor are they born with bombs in their hands. Even if we do not accept that their reasons justify their actions, we still need to determine what their reasons are. Only then can we work to alter the underlying conditions that made that step seem reasonable to them.

It is the reality that we are interdependent that makes it imperative that we not only look for ways to halt each new terrorist act but also to identify the causes and conditions that give rise to such violence. Interdependence also makes it possible to counteract those acts non-violently. By shifting even one of the causes and necessary conditions, we can and will change the end result. For that to happen, we must acknowledge and understand them.

BEFORE CASTING THE FIRST STONE

When we analyze the forces that motivate harmful behavior, we find a fairly familiar set of dark emotions, such as anger, jealousy, and greed. Like the very different emotions of love and compassion, these are inner conditions that impact our relationships with others, but in harmful rather than healthy ways. We need to understand our negative inner conditions so we can reduce them and base our connections with others on our positive qualities instead.

We fall prey to disturbing emotions that can overtake us and influence our judgment, our decisions, and our behavior. We can become totally controlled by disturbing emotions such as anger. To fully understand how anger works, let's begin with our own experience, for we all have experienced it at one point or other. When we look back on such moments, we might find that the disturbing emotion functioned like a kind of illness.

We can observe ourselves sometime after we have finished an angry outburst. When we were overtaken by anger, we may have broken things or said and done things that caused various kinds of damage. Later in a moment of relative calm, when we look back at ourselves as we were in the moment of rage, it can seem as if we had become someone else. During that onslaught of intense anger, we were no longer quite like a normal person, or even like ourselves. We say we were not in our right mind. In a sense, we were impaired like a person who is temporarily insane or whose empathy is completely switched off.

Sitting there amid the broken glass and other signs of our destructive anger, we might have good reason to fear ourselves! This is a good example for us to contemplate carefully and then apply to other people and see if it helps us to be more understanding and forgiving—and less quick to dismiss others as totally different from us.

If we are looking for the actual source of the violent behavior we see in the world, the blame should be laid squarely on the disturbing emotions that were present at the time of the action, not simply on the person as a whole. However, we do not usually approach anger and violence from this viewpoint. Normally we see the person as fundamentally flawed rather than finding fault with the disturbing emotion that led them to engage in such misguided and destructive actions.

I really want to stress that we are not seeking a deeper comprehension of such harmful behavior in order to justify or accept it. Learning to break a situation down into its constituent conditions and parts is necessary in order to see how things can be changed. It allows us to isolate, denounce, and eliminate the causes of the destructive behavior rather than rejecting or eliminating the person as a whole. We all fall prey to destructive emotions such as anger, at different moments and to different degrees. If we were to eliminate everyone who experienced strong anger at some point in their lives, we would have no one left in society. Therefore we need to improve our skills at reducing the emotion of anger individually and as a society.

Everyone is exactly equal in terms of not wanting suffering. We can see that some people are less effective than others at creating the causes for happiness and avoiding suffering. No one in their right mind actually seeks out pain and problems, yet we see people harming others or themselves and clearly not making any progress toward securing their own happiness and well-being.

When we observe this, we are observing someone even more worthy of our compassion, because they are digging themselves ever deeper into suffering and problems. They have become enslaved to their own disturbing emotions and lack true freedom. It can actually be painful to contemplate how terribly caught they have become in the prison they are creating for themselves. Even as we develop strategies for reducing negative conditions, we can also be actively working toward greater empathy for those who feel such harmful emotions.

In our quest to enhance our own empathy, we don't work only with those who deserve our pity. We can also work to connect empathetically with people who are seemingly better off than us, people toward whom we might otherwise experience envy or resentment. Rather than fixating on the differences between their situation and ours, we can recollect the shared aspiration that we all have.

Happiness is boundless. If wealthy people approach their pursuit of happiness as if it were something to acquire in parcels, they will never get enough. The resources that we all have in abundance are our inner resources, and these are what we can develop boundlessly to yield the happiness we yearn for. When we are focusing solely on material resources as a means of securing happiness, chances are we will not actually experience happiness but will feel we are in competition for limited resources.

As I have said, empathy does not require you to condone what others do or excuse it. It just gives you some understanding of what they are undergoing. With empathy, there can remain a certain sense of separation, where the other person is over there, and from where you are, you recognize what they feel or are experiencing. Subject and object are distinct or even distant. By contrast, compassion brings you closer. Compassion goes deeper than empathy and involves you further.

With compassion, you feel as if that distance disappears, and you imagine that you actually are the other person. It is as if you have gone to their place. You and they almost become one person. You can feel the other's suffering and wish for them to be free of it, as acutely as or even more acutely than she or he does. You can be willing and in fact eager to do whatever is necessary to ease their suffering.

Compassion is therefore more engaged and much more active than empathy alone. The emotional understanding that empathy gives us is certainly important, but with compassion you enter into the situation with body, speech, heart, and mind. You might pass someone on the street and feel some empathy, but compassion stops you in your tracks. It draws you in and much more readily translates into action.

We might start off with a basic understanding that generally all beings who have the capacity to feel pain and joy also wish for happiness and to escape suffering. This may initially be little more than an intellectual idea. We may have a general awareness that others wish to be free of their problems. However, if the person in question is our parent or our child, we do not leave it at the level of mere awareness. The emotional experience is stronger than with empathy, and we are moved to action. Where there is compassion, there is much more energy to act.

Although empathy can give us the awareness or understanding

of what the other is undergoing, the other somehow remains other. Compassion enters straight into your heart. There is not much sense of subject and object, and little separation. We are almost one person with them.

ENDING SPECTATOR COMPASSION

During the Boston Marathon bombing, I saw images of a young man with both legs blown off, his bones protruding, being assisted by an older man in a cowboy hat. When we watch the images from our safe distance, we might feel squeamish and discomfited by the sight of that injury. That compassion is a sort of spectator compassion. It is wholly unlike the compassion of the man in the cowboy hat. He was so totally focused on saving the younger man's life that there was no space for any sense of his own personal distress.

When you are completely connected to another's situation and feel as if you were in their place, you direct all your energy toward finding some solution—staunching the bleeding, keeping him calm so he does not go into shock, carrying him to where he can receive medical treatment—anything and everything you can possibly do to protect his life and ease his pain. Your thoughts and feelings are so completely directed toward addressing and ending that suffering that you only experience the wish to free him from suffering. You do not actually experience suffering.

For those of us still at the level of spectator compassion—which hardly deserves the name compassion—it is more like looking at a photograph. It is a kind of knowing without really feeling. But for the people actually feeling compassion, it is profoundly moving. Real compassion connects with the living experience and wants to move with the person, to bring them out of suffering and up to the final goal of happiness.

I think if your empathy with someone you see suffering overwhelms you with suffering yourself, this is a sign that you have not fully come over to the other's place. You are still a spectator of someone else's pain. Your empathy has not gone far enough. You see a hungry person begging for food. As a spectator, you can always look away or walk away. But the truly compassionate person cannot leave the other there suffering. They feel they must carry them if necessary until they find food. They cannot walk away from their hunger.

This is the irony of compassion: when your awareness of others' suffering remains mere knowledge without full affective involvement, it can cause you pain and distress. Once you connect completely on the level of feelings, that distress goes away.

To support our cultivation of compassion, we can also adjust where we direct our attention. This is another inner condition we can work with. As I described in my earlier book *The Heart Is Noble,* the focus of our compassion should not be narrowly aimed at the suffering itself but must take in the person who is suffering. If our attention is completely occupied by the suffering, we lose sight of the person him or herself, and fall into feelings of helplessness at the prospect of having to eliminate the problems that loom so large in our awareness. When we are connecting with the person in their pain, we do not even consider this option of giving up and abandoning them in that state.

COURAGE IS THE ROOT OF COMPASSION

The element of courage is essential for strengthening our empathy. Empathy might stand by helplessly, but compassion does not leave you feeling overwhelmed or impotent in the face of the suffering you see. Compassion means you have the strong aspiration and in fact a firm resolve to do something to end the suffering.

Courage is the root of compassion. With compassion, you need to be able to envision the end goal—the happiness that you want the other to attain. It is not the case that when you feel compassion you only see suffering and pain and cannot see anything beyond that. Rather, you have the imagination to see the other as free and happy, and you keep that aim in mind.

With compassion, the result—happiness—is present before you, like a finish line. In a race, you might be tired physically, but you are sustained by your determination not to stop until you have reached your final goal. You are sustained by joy at the prospect of attaining that goal.

SIX

Opening Heart and Mind

OUR ERA OF CONNECTIVITY poses particular challenges to keeping our heart and mind open. We are exposed to so many images and reports of violence and misery that we feel as if we ourselves are being bombarded. It is a common experience when watching the news on the TV or computer screen to feel that all the suffering we see is being transmitted to us, making us suffer ourselves. Our response is often to shut down. Thinking, "I can't take any more suffering. I need to protect my own happiness," we change to another channel or webpage.

But the suffering in the world is still out there, and by turning away from it, we are not truly protecting ourselves. On the contrary, we are harming ourselves, because we are damaging immeasurably valuable resources within us, resources that we urgently need to protect in order to live well in an interdependent world.

The damage is not done by the news of suffering. The real damage is done by our own hardening of heart to that suffering. We harm ourselves when we close ourselves off from others. This makes it especially important that we actively work to keep our mind and heart open, for our own sake and for the benefit of others.

I was born into a Buddhist family that valued a warm and open heart. Later, once I was recognized as the Karmapa and taken to the monastery, it was communicated to me in many different ways that I must keep myself completely open and attentive to others' needs and feelings. Tremendous emphasis was placed throughout my upbringing on the importance of having an open mind and heart that feels genuine concern and responsibility for others. Given the role that I would play as Karmapa, this training with the ultimate aim of being able to keep the heart completely open, all the time, to everyone, equally, was considered an extremely important part of my education.

Extending one's self to others in this way is truly noble and valuable, but it is certainly not easy to do. Yet it is a goal worth seeking even if we do not succeed fully. Every effort to extend ourselves to others with heart and mind open is worthwhile, because it helps us to develop qualities that are of immense value in life.

TRUST AS A GIFT

Sometimes people hurt us, or we anticipate that they might act against our interests if we give them the opportunity. These moments pose some of the biggest challenges to keeping our heart and mind open. People seem to assume that because I live in the apparently sheltered world of a Buddhist monastery, I face no such issues in the cultivation of a wide open heart. While the particulars of my life situation are quite different from those of most everyone else, everyone's life poses challenges to keeping one's mind and heart open. I have certainly encountered obstacles, too. In fact, my life might even offer more challenges than average in that regard.

I have numerous responsibilities as a spiritual leader within Tibetan Buddhism. In order to fulfill those responsibilities and engage in my religious activities, I depend on many people and have become connected with numerous people in relationships of mutual dependency. They depend on me and I depend on them. Yet because of how closely integrated Buddhism is into Tibetan culture as a whole, and for numerous historical reasons, politics and religion are mixed in Tibetan society. Within my environment, all these elements come into play: religious and social concerns, but political ones too. When such interests enter into the picture, it can be very challenging to stay open and trusting. Political interests can lead to partisan thinking and competitive behavior.

By contrast, as a spiritual leader engaging in altruistic activities, it is part of my training to extend myself unconditionally and unreservedly toward all others, holding nothing back. However, I am warned by well-meaning people not to be so trusting. They have my interests at heart when they warn me that some of those around me are abusing their relationship with me, exploiting me or my name for their own personal aims. In fact, these are not simply paranoid warnings. Many of the people around me have pure altruistic interests and sincere intentions. Yet there is a possibility that some may approach me out of political or personal interests. This can happen and indeed has happened on numerous occasions.

There have been people I trusted who did not fully live up to the trust placed in them, and who have taken advantage of the care and concern I showed them. There were cases where people spoke ill of me behind my back and approached me subsequent to that, pretending to be fully supportive and sincere. I was aware of these actions, but that is no reason for me to adopt similar behavior. These people need something of me and depend on me to give it to them, and there will be ways I can help them. Since my commitment is to do what is beneficial for them, I can hold to that as the guiding principle in how I respond to their requests of me.

There is no point in getting angry in such cases, feeling bitter, or bearing a grudge. This serves no purpose whatsoever. There is truly no reason to reciprocate with similar treatment. Just because others are not open toward you does not mean you have to shut them out or withdraw your basic benevolent attitude. Therefore I do not confront them with what I know of their duplicity but simply help them in whatever way I can. I may not always meet their expectations or please them, but I seek never to harm them and to benefit them as much as I can.

From my side, I offer trust. My trust is unconditional. I simply do not wish to base it on how others behave. In that sense, there is no reason for my trust: it is an unconditional gift. I am not engaging in barter for trust—"If you do this for me, you can cash it in for my trust." Trust is something I place in others freely, out of what you might call the goodness of my heart.

But this does not mean you hand your bank account details over to a stranger. That would be taking it much too far. Trust does not mean you invite others to take advantage of you during the give and take of our ordinary transactions in life. Rather, to trust means that you will show them whatever purity you have. If they present you with something dirty, since you do not want it, you do not need to take it on. You can just keep to your own pure principles. There can be some inner qualities that you simply do not want to subject to external conditions and that you are willing to go to great lengths to guard. For me, trust is one of those.

Our own goodness and purity are far too valuable to compromise in the face of relatively less important matters. Personally, I see it as vastly more important to protect one's open-hearted altruism and one's open-minded goodness than to protect any shorter-term interests. To protect oneself means to protect one's own pure nature. This is the most important protection we can give ourselves, and protecting ourselves this way also protects others.

While the altruistic openness of heart and mind is other-oriented, at the same time it enriches us incalculably as well. It benefits oneself and others simultaneously. This is one important effect of living in harmony with the principle of interdependence: the sense of hard opposition between self and others softens.

CULTIVATING RADICAL OPENNESS

The capacity to truly see and stay open to others when they are suffering has to be developed gradually. We cannot rush this process. If we try to open ourselves too much, too quickly, we risk becoming overwhelmed and shutting down altogether. We might decide that others' suffering is so far beyond our ability to address that we just turn away, telling ourselves that this concept of an open heart and mind is just too hard and too idealistic, and has no pragmatic effect anyway.

We hear in the news that millions of children in Africa have died of malaria in this year alone, millions of Syrians have been driven from their homes by war, or that thousands of people have died in a single flood. If we are not careful how we approach it, this can seem so immense that you yourself feel tiny and weak in the face of it, as if you were watching a huge typhoon from inside a tiny hut.

We have to consciously—and carefully—build up our ability to stay open to the sufferings of others. From my own experience, I can assure you that if you train gradually to extend your care each day just a little bit more than before, your capacity to stay open will improve slowly over time. The more you stick with it, the more openness of heart and mind becomes a part of you—and the bigger a part of you it can become.

As we think about what inner conditions would help us develop more openness, we find that patience serves as an important supportive inner condition in the cultivation of this and many other qualities. Our task at hand involves bringing together the conditions within ourselves, so that they strengthen each other and allow us to keep building toward a universal sense of compassion. Ultimately, we will work toward a sense of universal responsibility as well, as we will discuss later. These are very long-term goals that will require patience to keep working toward until we reach them.

Along the way, we must guard carefully against falling into a habit of justifying our indifference in the face of others' suffering. This is a very serious obstacle not only to the possibility of creating a healthy global society but also to living a healthy human life.

It can help to make conscious efforts to simply hold the person suffering in our awareness. This alone can strengthen our determination and our courage to act. Such determination and courage protect us against the apathy that can arise when we feel overwhelmed by the complexity or immensity of a problem. We must ensure that we never end up looking for excuses to do nothing about others' suffering.

UNIVERSAL AND UNCONDITIONAL

As in any gradual training process, at the beginning we will find it is easier to stay open to some people than to others. As I mentioned, some people might find that they connect more readily with animals than humans. Certainly there will be some people we open to almost effortlessly, and others that require concerted effort. This is quite normal, and we can start from there. This need not pose a problem. It only becomes one when we stop expanding our capacity to feel connected, leaving others outside the walls of our own ego-centered world.

It is a basic fact that anyone who has consciousness has the capacity to feel pain and experience happiness and joy. We all share this same profound wish to be happy. If we reflect deeply on this fact, it is clear that we have no valid basis for including some in the embrace of our compassion while excluding others.

Not only are we all equal, we are also ultimately connected to all beings with whom we share the planet through the numberless interconnections that link us all. When we look through the lens of interdependence, as we have discussed, the strong walls that we imagine separating ourselves from others are revealed to be mere mental projections, and ultimately unsustainable. When we recognize how thoroughly we are shaped by our connections to countless others, we can come to know and feel that others truly are part of us and that we are part of them.

Even when we are able to extend our compassion to many beings, as long as there are walls that separate us from some beings, there are still walls around us. As long as there are beings who suffer whom we have left out, we have not yet developed our compassion to its full capacity. Interdependence encourages us to aspire to ultimately be able to respond to all equally with universal compassion and accept the responsibility for their well-being.

A sense of universal responsibility for the whole world is not something that springs forth full-blown. It is something that we must continually orient ourselves toward. Even though we cannot benefit everyone all at once, as our altruistic orientation becomes more stable, when we see an opportunity to be of help to someone, we will be ready to seize it. We will have trained ourselves to be fully open and available to others.

Even if we do not reach the goal of caring for all beings, every effort we make to open that widely has a profound impact on us. It is a goal so noble that it is worth cultivating even if we never manage to fulfill it.

A BRAVE HEART

A great deal of courage is required in order to keep our minds and hearts open. Courage and openness of heart together form a powerful support for acting on our compassion. Compassion implies the feeling that "I will do what is needed to free those afflicted by suffering from their pains and problems." This attitude has an element of determination, joined with hope or strong aspiration that it can be done, combined with the courage to act to accomplish it oneself.

Compassion is not passive or helpless. It is not an attitude of pity, thinking "What a shame that these people are suffering but that is just the way it is, and there is nothing much to be done about it." With real compassion, even if you see nothing to be done at that moment, you do not withdraw your concern. In fact, you reinforce it with the resolution to keep looking until you find a way to ease their pain.

Your heart must be able to stay open until that moment comes. You need an open mind as well, to maintain a state of mental readiness and agility to respond appropriately to whatever opportunities arise to ease others' suffering. This implies training until your compassion is universal and can be enacted toward anyone at all.

For our compassion to become universal, we must teach our heart to be radically open and radically inclusive. Not a single being is left outside. Human or animal, no matter how large or small, no matter how many or how few, since there is no difference in their wish to be happy, we do not exclude them from our compassion and care. It does not matter whether we know them or not. We know that they share the same existential condition as us. The courage of an open heart is key.

FACING OUR FEARS

Universal open-heartedness and compassion excludes no one whatsoever. We can enlist our imagination as a supportive condition in cultivating this noble attitude. We could imagine a tiger coming to attack us and envision ways to stay connected with compassion for this being who is driven by hunger and rapidly losing its territory to human encroachment. We can be creative and think up any scenario that allows us to keep a connection of compassion alive in our heart and mind. Perhaps we imagine we are a villager feeling great compassion while we safely trap the tiger and call the authorities to take it to a better habitat. Perhaps we imagine ourselves as a Buddhist monk and try to feel what it would be like to meditate on compassion even as the tiger approaches to eat us. Actually, there was a conservationist who spontaneously sat down once when he turned and saw that a jaguar was following him in a jungle in Central America. He had dedicated his life to protecting and studying jaguars and, suddenly faced with one in the flesh, amid his fear he also preserved the wish to connect with it. To his surprise and delight, the jaguar also sat down and they remained for a time just observing each other before each went their separate way. As a mental exercise, we could imagine ourselves in the same scenario.

Who knows how we might actually respond if we were caught in the gaze of a fierce predator, but the point is to prepare ourselves in advance to respond with compassion toward absolutely anyone we encounter.

To bring it closer to home, we might ask ourselves what we would feel if a lone wolf terrorist, or maybe an acknowledged member of ISIS, suddenly arrived in our midst. How would we look at him? Would we be able to recollect that he feels pain and is trying somehow to find his way to happiness? It is important to ask ourselves this and prepare ourselves to keep in sight our shared existential condition, no matter how radically different our ways of dealing with our specific life conditions may be.

Working with the fears that make it hard for us to open up and remain so is an integral part of learning to live a healthy interdependent life. Fear can keep us from growing beyond what is familiar and comfortable for us.

I can speak of this from my experience leaving Tibet. Even though Tibet is ruled by the Chinese, which brings its own problems, the fact remains that I was familiar with that environment. When I escaped to India seeking freedom, I left behind my family as well as all the rest of what I knew and had grown familiar with. Though I have personally gained tremendously in many ways by coming here, I cannot say I have gained in terms of a sense of ease or comfort. However, I have no cause whatsoever for regret. It has been far more beneficial for me to be in India than to have stayed in Tibet. I have been able to do and learn so much and have met so many people I would never have been able to meet had I stayed within my comfort zone. Comparing the loss of comfort and familiarity to the gain in wisdom and growth, it is of far greater advantage to face our fear of the unknown and venture outside our comfort zones.

FROM RESULTS TO CAUSES

We need not do anything so drastic as fleeing to another country in order to grow. We do not need new physical territory to gain fresh perspectives. We can open up new vistas, and make powerful inner changes, just by altering our way of seeing our situation. One such shift is to focus on the causes that create situations rather than the situation that results from those causes. This is a subtle but powerful change in perspective.

Living our life as if it were a procession of results we must face is neither productive nor necessary. When we are fully aware of interdependence, we know that we can create the results we want by identifying and then creating the causes and conditions that bring about those results. We can end unwanted situations by eliminating their causes. To live interdependence is to live as a conscious agent of change.

We can do this for our own situations and for those of others. In the course of strengthening our compassion, I have mentioned moving our attention so that the person is firmly in our gaze, avoiding focusing entirely on the suffering. Another powerful change takes place when we shift our attention away from the suffering that a person is experiencing as a result of some inner or outer conditions and focus instead on the conditions themselves.

As the law of causality teaches us, when suffering is present, it is a result of various causes and conditions that have come together. When confronted by others' suffering, we can of course offer comfort and encouragement, but what we most want is to actually eliminate their suffering. To end suffering, we need to work with its causes and conditions. Therefore we widen our lens to bring into sharp focus the underlying causes and conditions, rather than just seeing the outcome. Like physicians, we look behind the symptoms, seeking to diagnose the disease and identify its underlying causes.

This reorientation can be applied to any problem we wish to address. No matter how huge or solid a problem may seem, we can always break it down by undertaking a causal analysis. Indeed, to change any situation in life or in the world, we must first examine its causes. From there we can discover where we as agents of change can make a difference.

Take global warming, for example, and think about it as if it were a result—as something that has already come about. It can appear to be such a solid and huge problem that we can neither escape it nor even face it squarely. It appears to be immense and overwhelming. However, if we look at global warming in terms of its causes and conditions, we can identify specific actions and human behaviors that contributed to its arising. This makes it clear that many distinct conditions all converged to create the situation we now have. Changing any one of those conditions can subtly change the outcome. When you have changed enough conditions, the situation shifts. Climate change may seem to be taking place up there in the sky, but many of its causes are right down here on the earth in human hands.

The key step is to bring our awareness of climate change down to earth as well. This happens by increasing our emotional engagement with what we are learning, until we are moved to act. For example, we may have read that certain types of food, such as meat, are particularly intensive in their consumption of water. But there is a different sort of knowledge that arises when we listen to a brook whose flow has dwindled to a trickle or imagine the thirst of plants that have withered in the parched earth—or when we disconnect our hoses and haul buckets to water our garden by hand. Once we feel our connectedness to the systems we are part of, the step to action follows much more naturally.

When we feel deeply moved by a problem, we discover a great deal we can do to affect the outcome, even when the problem is as complex as climate change. Human beings face many such painful situations and endemic social ills where numerous different conditions would have to be changed in order to end the suffering. But not all forms of suffering are so difficult to address. Many forms of human and animal suffering we could dispel with relative ease. This is another reason we need to keep an open mind, able to see things from various angles, so that we can identify the contributing conditions that may be shifted. Sometimes it turns out to be far easier than we anticipate.

FOCUSING ON MOTIVATION

The world we are sharing in the twenty-first century is a place of great diversity. To keep our hearts and minds open to others whose cultural assumptions and expectations vary widely from our own, we must be able to value and genuinely respect that diversity. We need to feel our equality without wishing that others would conform to some unstated norm, as we explored in the chapter on equality and difference. If we judge others as wanting and shut them out from our concern and care, we might well be falling prey to the same closed-mindedness or intolerance for which we are faulting them. Keeping a clear-sighted view of the basis of our equality and the importance of diversity helps us keep our heart and mind open.

A few years after I arrived in India from Tibet, I became vegetarian. I held the firm conviction that eating meat was harmful to animals and to the planet, and this moved me to give up meat completely. At that time there were people around me who continued to eat meat, and in fact enjoyed doing so.

In one way perhaps it is difficult to understand that people near a Buddhist spiritual leader who promotes vegetarianism would feel comfortable continuing to eat meat. But looking from another angle, I could understand them. Shifting to a vegetarian diet is a huge step for Tibetans. Our way of life for millennia has relied heavily on meat, in part because the fragile biosphere of the Tibetan plateau did not lend itself to a diverse food supply.

Some questioned the fact that I was willing to have such people around me. What most seemed to trouble those who held this opinion was the outer behavior, not the inner orientation. However, for me it is important to become vegetarian from a feeling, grounded in understanding, that giving up meat is really worthwhile.

When we act in line with our personal values, we must take care not to do so with pride or conceit, otherwise our attitude undermines the value of our conduct. All our actions, attitudes, and motivations interact, and each is impacted by the other. This is a reflection of interdependence. If we are not careful, our arrogance can take our positive qualities and actions and use them to inflate our prideful disdain.

It can happen that we feel superior to others because we are vegetarian. But in giving up meat all we have really done is avoided committing an error. We recognize that eating meat is harmful, so we correct our mistake and are doing something that benefits ourselves and others. It is nothing to blow out of proportion, build an identity on, or become prideful about. Sometimes I joke a bit with meat-eaters

I know about their meat-eating, but otherwise it is not something to make an issue of. Actually, there is nothing special about being vegetarian. I've heard that Hitler was vegetarian. Clearly, being vegetarian is not an irrefutable sign that you are a good person.

What I am saying is this: Our change in behavior should come from an emotional awareness of the effect of our actions on others. If we recognize the pain and suffering we cause to beings when they are killed in order for us to consume their flesh and we feel a wish to stop inflicting this torment on them, and therefore we give up meat, that is a significant act. This would be a sign we have made the needed shift from understanding to feeling to acting based on an awareness of our interdependence. But if we are simply imitating the behavior of others or following a trend, then that is not a very meaningful transformation. Of course, the animals we are not eating benefit greatly from our act of giving up their meat, and that alone is worthwhile. But it is not as if being vegetarian makes us essentially better than those who eat meat. Certainly it is nothing to brag about. Nor should we use our vegetarianism to make those who eat meat feel inferior.

We can make a show so that others see us as open-minded and open-hearted. But an open heart and mind is an inner orientation toward the needs of others. Although that orientation definitely leads to actions that can be observed from the outside, it is not primarily a matter of changing our conduct but of extending ourselves to others fully, in heart, mind, and action.

A LONG-TERM VIEW

Gaining wisdom about the interplay of motivations, perceptions, feelings, and actions helps us navigate our interactions with others more wisely. A commitment to openness reminds us to be cautious in how we interpret others' behavior toward us. We cannot deduce others' motivations simply from their words and physical gestures, because people are moved by inner forces that we cannot perceive directly. Generally, when we place so much emphasis on the physical, we miss or misread a great deal of what people actually hold in their hearts and minds.

Living in an increasingly globalized society makes this point particularly acute. Not only are we interacting with people whose emotional and mental state is obscure to us, we are often connecting with them across cultural differences. Because we have internalized differing cultural norms, and are responding from within differing social expectations and material circumstances, the external expression of our inner states is bound to look very different.

Even the dynamics of the closest relationships—such as that between parent and child—are shaped by cultural conditioning. In the eyes of Tibetans, Western parents seem tremendously generous and kind, giving children the freedom to act however they wish, endeavoring to buy them whatever they ask for, and generally seeking to satisfy their child's whims. Tibetan parents say "no" far more often than they say "yes." They do so even when they can afford to indulge the child's appetites, apparently as a matter of principle. In fact, Tibetan parents seem eager to ensure that children not only understand that they cannot have everything they want but also discourage them from spending energy trying to get more. Western parents and children repeatedly hug and kiss, and explicitly tell each other, "I love you." Tibetan parents, by contrast, might never verbalize that feeling in words. Surely there are cultural differences at work here. We cannot conclude from this that parents in one culture love their children more than in another.

Curiously, though, as adults, it is not uncommon for Westerners to have very mixed feelings toward their parents and question their motivations. I occasionally hear comments from Westerners to the effect that they feel their parents' love for them is not unconditional but merely conditional upon their pleasing them—getting good grades, meeting their standards of behavior and success, and so on. In the case of Tibetans, the question of whether or not they have their parents' love never seems to arise. Somehow as adults Tibetans generally have no doubt that there was real affection underlying their parents' treatment of them. They feel loved by their parents though they may never have heard the words "I love you" from them even once. It is as if a confidence in their parents' love for them unfolds gradually and subtly over time.

When we harbor too many expectations of how people should treat us verbally and physically, we may fail to recognize the real concern for us that they feel in their hearts. This may be due to differences in cultural norms or individual personality. Some parents simply have rougher manners than others; others find it hard to express their emotions. They may fear being seen to be vulnerable. There can be many reasons for others' warmth to feel cold to us.

Sometimes it helps to take a long-term view. That might just reveal that what you were observing was love, expressed perhaps not as you hoped but as the conditions—personal, cultural, and otherwise— permitted. The ever-present possibility of discovering that things are not as we had thought is always there. We just need to stay open.

SEVEN

Authentic Freedom

FREEDOM IS a powerful idea. But I am not sure we are always very clear what we have in mind when we speak of it. Does freedom mean doing whatever we feel like in any given moment? Does it mean having the power and liberty to exercise our will with no obstruction? Does it evoke a state in which we have shed ourselves of all obligations to others?

Many of our notions of freedom are based implicitly on the idea that we are utterly self-sustaining and separate entities. This model leads us to feel that others' claims on us undercut our freedom. We experience our relationships as ties that bind us and limit our freedom. Based on this, we assume that we cannot all be free, because the freedom of one person comes at the cost of another's. If we believe that, it is small wonder that people so often seek to dominate and oppress others. This is an idea that slips into discussions of freedom—the idea that freedom is in some fundamental way a limited resource, such that one person exercising his freedom detracts from another person's ability to be free. But this is not the case. Freedom is not a zero-sum game.

It *is* possible and realistic for every person to experience real freedom. The reason we have not managed to do so is we lack an understanding of what real freedom is and how it can be achieved. We need the wisdom to distinguish the egocentric pursuit of self-interest from the pursuit of authentic freedom.

When I hear what people say about freedom sometimes, it sounds to me like longing to live out the fantasy of being independent and absolutely autonomous individuals, of being free of consequences and responsibilities—that is to say, exempt from the principle of interdependence. But there is no such thing. We cannot exist outside causality or outside the connections of interdependence, and so freedom cannot be a matter of escaping from those connections.

Only freedom developed on the basis of a realistic view of who we are and how we relate to others can be authentic—and extended universally to all. If we acknowledge our interdependence, and take into account the vast networks of interconnections in which our lives and actions are embedded, we will find that our own freedom is inseparable from the freedom of all other people. When we truly appreciate this fact, we experience interdependent freedom—a freedom that does not detract from others' freedom. This is the freedom that we can all enjoy together without conflict.

FREEDOM'S INNER CONDITIONS

Freedom does not start from the outside. Although external conditions have a part to play, that is not where freedom originates. This might sound backward, but authentic freedom arises initially from inner conditions. Its deepest roots are within us.

Most often when we speak of freedom, what we actually have in mind are freedom's outer manifestations. This may be the gravest error we make in our understanding of freedom. If we think we will achieve freedom when we can exercise complete control over our immediate environment, we overlook the single most important determinant of authentic freedom: our own minds.

Our mind has unlimited potential. It is not bound to any one position or viewpoint. What we think or feel—our mental state—is not simply determined by outer circumstances. Because of this, no matter how challenging our external conditions might be, we can experience freedom if we cultivate the inner resources that allow us to feel free. The basis for establishing authentic freedom is within us.

If you can access a sense of inner freedom no matter what is going on around you, you are experiencing freedom. As important as outer liberties are, freedom does not consist solely in enjoying physical or verbal liberty, such as freedom of movement or freedom of speech. We may have the liberty to do and say as we wish and yet still be deeply unfree mentally or emotionally. This is why inner freedom is key. When we have freed our minds and hearts from within, our happiness no longer depends on making the rest of the world serve our self-centered goals. Not only that, we gain freedom to work to change the external conditions that have the potential to limit or obstruct our freedom from outside, and we also have what we need to be able to work for the freedom of others.

What are we looking for when we seek freedom? Maybe at the bottom of it all, the freedom we seek is the experience of genuine happiness. Since this is an inner experience, external things cannot be the measure of our happiness or our freedom. We will come back in a moment to the question of what we mean by happiness and how it enables us to experience freedom, but I think if we examine our own experiences, we can see that whether we call it freedom or not, if we feel free, we feel happy, and if we feel happy, we also feel free. The state of mind and the feeling we seek can be called freedom, or it can be called happiness. But whatever name we give it, if we want to experience happiness or freedom, we must cultivate the inner conditions that give rise to those states.

Let us take a look at some of the expectations that arise when we focus outward when thinking about freedom. If we define freedom as disentangling ourselves entirely from all connection to and responsibility for others, that moment will never come; our connections form part of us and therefore we cannot leave them behind. If we define freedom as ridding ourselves of external constraints and controlling our surroundings, we are also doomed to fail. For even if we could get all external conditions exactly as we wish them, it is impossible to keep them that way indefinitely.

The Tibetan term for freedom is literally "self-control" or "self-mastery." We have a saying, "Being in control of oneself is happiness; being controlled by what is other is suffering." What this is pointing out is that when we have self-mastery, we have access to happiness. All forms of being overpowered by others—other people or other forces, external or internal—are sources of suffering. If we have mastery over ourselves, we can be happy. If we do not have self-mastery, we will suffer.

If we do not consider internal as well as external constraints, we may take this to suggest that freedom means not being subject to any external authority. But we can also fall victim to inner forces that take over and control us. We can lose our freedom to the obsessive emotional states of jealousy, anger, and attachment. If we can physically go where we wish and speak our minds any time we wish, yet we are living out of control, at the whim of whatever our own disturbing emotional states tell us to do, say, or think, then we are not truly free, are we? If we are slaves to inner masters of greed, resentment, or prejudice, that is hardly full freedom. Freeing ourselves from those inner masters is required to experience authentic freedom.

To explore this, we can ask, if someone hits us with a stick, are we angry at the stick or at the person hitting us? This question might seem absurd, but breaking it down logically, it is the stick that directly caused us pain. However, we know the stick is not in control, and so we do not direct our anger at the stick. Like us, the stick is a victim in this scenario. We likewise don't blame the hand wielding the stick. Rather, we look to the person controlling the hand. This seems logical to us. Yet the person himself or herself was overpowered by anger and driven to act by their rage. Following this line of reflection, logic should lead us to recognize that the locus of power is not the person but the emotional forces that have taken control from within. The person attacking us fell under the control of their anger, just as has surely happened to us on occasion.

What this shows is that we can lose our freedom in many ways. Even when we have external freedoms like freedom of speech, freedom of movement, and the freedom to gather, we may still be mentally or emotionally overpowered. We could still be controlled by disturbing emotions whose orders we are executing. This lack of inner freedom curtails our ability to feel content, to make wise choices, and to make the most of our external freedoms.

For this reason, authentic freedom must include freedom from the control of destructive emotional forces. In this area, we gain greater freedom by actively training ourselves. Achieving inner freedom entails hard work, but it can be consciously cultivated. Here, again, our intelligence is a powerful tool. We can apply it with wisdom and patience to understand how our destructive emotions work so that we can gradually liberate ourselves from their dictates.

You are already taking the first step right now, by reflecting on how emotional forces work in order to determine which are constructive and helpful and which are destructive and harmful. From there, you can learn how the destructive ones work so that you can enter into dialogue with them and get them to release their hold on you. You can learn that you do not need to do their bidding. In each step of this process, you are freeing yourself from their power over you.

For example, when you feel strong anger toward someone, what often happens is that you ruminate and ponder ways to bring them down. But before you ever harm them, you have already harmed yourself. You lose sleep. You are eaten up inside by anger and lose your appetite. Your health suffers. This is profoundly unwise.

When you fuel your anger, you have already made yourself your first victim. You come under the sway of a cruel master who takes away your freedom and makes you hurt yourself. Recognizing that is the first step toward self-mastery.

BENEFITS OF SELF-DISCIPLINE

Self-mastery entails self-discipline, but neither self-mastery nor self-discipline is a matter of applying superior force. It is not like a parent pushing a child to do her homework long enough that she finally grudgingly does it to avoid being scolded by her parents. Self-discipline can be developed joyfully rather than as a burden we impose on ourselves. It can become something we willingly embrace. This requires training—mind training.

We need to recognize that our minds are big enough and can open wide enough to accept reality. We need to talk to our minds. The aim is for us to choose, wholeheartedly, to do what we know is the best thing to do.

I am not speaking as someone unfamiliar with the experience of being encumbered by the obligations of roles that must be fulfilled. Just as people with a normal life sometimes want to be famous, public figures sometimes yearn for something more normal. Sometimes I wish I could live as a normal monk or a normal Tibetan. Even His Holiness the Pope can announce that he believes the time has come for the next pope and simply resign his position. I do not have that option. I will always be the Karmapa.

When I feel constricted, I cannot just resign. But I can talk to myself and ask my mind, "Please, open a bit more."

We sometimes forget that we have the freedom to work with our own minds. When I find myself in moments like the one I describe, I try to remember that no one is in control of my mind but me and work with it to open further.

ABUNDANT FREEDOM AND HAPPINESS

I hope it is clear that in speaking of inner freedom, I do not mean freedom to follow emotional impulses or a temporary sense of release from restriction. Nor is it a matter of some ineffable feeling that comes or goes for no apparent reason. Our inner resources for consciously creating freedom run much deeper than that.

Freedom is rooted in wisdom. It involves an intelligent application of discernment conjoined with a sense of contentment—the ability to appreciate what we already have. I understand that this definition may challenge some of our more romantic notions of what freedom and happiness look like. It certainly departs from the model of freedom based on the concept of an independent, self-contained individual.

This is something I have learned from my own experience. As a public figure, I am not at liberty to rush out and indulge my whims without immediate consequences to many others. If the mood takes me, for example, I cannot just go outside and start up a basketball game in the monastery courtyard as an expression of my freedom. This may seem quite strange to many of you. After all, what is the big deal about getting a basketball game going? Given the circumstances of my life, it would be highly disruptive to numerous people, including the monks who help to maintain the traditional order of life in the monastery. The Indian and Tibetan security officers assigned to keep me safe would be obliged to follow me out there and clear the area of people. There are protocols they would have to follow. Additionally, as a spiritual leader responsible for heading a Buddhist order, I am expected to offer a model of the decorum of a monk for other monks and lay people.

Since my freedom and indeed my well-being are interconnected with that of many other people, rather than acting on my impulses, it makes far more sense for me to apply my intelligence and reflect that in fact I could just as easily be contented staying indoors, engaged in interesting conversation or spending my time some other way.

Playing basketball is just one of many possible experiences I could enjoy if I am looking for recreation. Neither freedom nor happiness is dependent upon enjoying one particular set of external conditions or having one particular experience. Freedom and happiness as opportunities are not one fixed thing.

A wise application of intelligence allows me to see that I am not confined to just one possibility. Discernment shows me that many other opportunities are also open to me. Patience helps me to keep a longer view, to see beyond the desire for instant gratification. Maintaining an open heart and mind helps me stay open to these other choices I can make. It helps me stay mentally flexible and able to find contentment and satisfaction in what I *do* have and *can* experience rather than fixating on what is beyond my reach. Thus multiple inner qualities work together to create a state of authentic freedom.

As an interdependent individual, my pursuit and experience of freedom need to take others into account as well. Freedom might help us better appreciate our equality. Freedom—like every other human experience—is carried out in a context of interdependence. Thus it inevitably depends on and involves many other people. For this reason, I can never validly say my freedom or happiness is more important than that of anyone else. We are equal. Therefore you are fully deserving of my respect, understanding, and empathy. I cannot disregard your freedom and well-being in pursuit of my own comfort or freedom.

Even in practical terms, disregarding others does not work because it goes against not only our equality but also our basic interdependence. This is why we need our capacity to experience contentment so that we can appreciate what we have rather than focusing on other possibilities. I am important, and others are important too. Others' happiness and freedom is every bit as important as mine, so when I stay indoors having a chat and let other people enjoy the space in the courtyard, I can truly feel that that is perfectly fine.

Freedom can be achieved amid interdependence and should not be confused with the momentary gratification of ego-centered impulses. Authentic freedom is rooted in an understanding of and respect for interdependence. It arises when we bring together the inner conditions that work interdependently within us to allow us to experience true freedom. These inner conditions that we have been discussing include such affective and cognitive capacities as discernment, empathy, openness, patience, wisdom, and contentment. These are values of interdependence and gain their value in part because they make true freedom possible.

INNER OCCUPATION

I have been emphasizing the importance of inner conditions for creating freedom, but this is not to deny the role of outer conditions in our ability to free ourselves. Nor does it mean that finding our own freedom is enough.

Our work for freedom does not end when we have freed our own minds. We start by focusing on inner freedom because it is a condition that we generally overlook and because it is the decisive condition, allowing us both to protect ourselves against external forces that would limit our own freedom and to be able to fight for freedom for others.

First we need to liberate our own mind. For example, if we want to fight against discrimination against women, we must first free ourselves from it. If in some subtle way we feel women are inferior, then our own mind is not free. If we are not free, how can we effectively fight for freedom? We might well end up perpetuating subtler forms of discrimination. When our own mind is free, we have the basis from which to fight for true freedom for others.

When we do not work consciously and actively to free our own mind, it can be as if our mind has been invaded and occupied. We might not even detect the conditions that are oppressing us and that need to be changed. Earlier we discussed the impact of communications technology and consumerist culture on our lives and on global society, and I think they also impact our freedom in different ways. These two external forces can limit our freedoms if we are not conscious of how we engage with them.

On the one hand, social media is a powerful forum for the exercise of free speech and the Internet clearly does facilitate a free exchange of ideas. We need only look at the example of the Arab Spring in 2011 to see the enormous potential of our connectivity in mobilizing collective action for freedom.

On the other hand, I think we can agree that electronic media are controlling our freedom in numerous but subtle ways, especially in combination with our global consumer culture. We may think we are free but actually be controlled by something else. We are bombarded by so much hype and spin that our ability to discern the world around us can be harmed.

The consumerist vision of happiness and success is projected online so skillfully and consistently that we do not realize it is just one possible vision. Multinational corporations hire the best experts they can find so they can make the most effective use of these media to convince us that we need their products or services. Smaller special interest groups invest heavily to find ways to promote their own vested concerns. Even ISIS is renowned for its adept use of electronic media. Information can be manipulated, and often is, and we in turn can be manipulated because we are disposed to believe in it.

Even from the relatively remote mountain area I live in, thirteen hours north of Delhi, I can see that technology can impinge on our freedom. Despite all the convenience of having a cell phone, you do lose a measure of privacy. I do not have a cell phone myself, but almost everyone I know does. They constantly report to one another where they are, where they are going next, and what they are doing. Privacy is such that nowadays, two people may feel they are having a very confidential conversation, but they might as well be broadcasting their words to the world. There is no guarantee that no one else is listening in.

Since September 11, while it is true that there are reasons to be more alert, we have also lost a great deal of privacy—a great deal more than necessary, I suspect. Our fears and anxieties can be used to control us, and before long we become willing to have our freedom invaded. We can even be persuaded to invite the invasion in. Focusing so much on external protection can make our minds more vulnerable to fear and hatred, which in the long run pose a greater threat to us than the terrorists we imagine around us. This is why it is so essential that the work to protect our external freedoms includes internal protection, by working with our own minds.

We need this internal protection so we can sustain the long-term work necessary to bring conditions of freedom to others. Creating freedom is not a matter of gaining a better quality of life for ourselves or embracing romantic notions of living on our own in an idyllic fantasy land. We share the world with people whose external conditions are horrifyingly lacking in freedom. There are people who are living as slaves, especially women; children of poor families are sold into servitude every day. When people lack the most basic external conditions of freedom—such as freedom of movement, freedom of self-determination, and freedom of religion—they are suffering indeed. We can and must concern ourselves with the outer conditions of people's freedom.

I have said this already, but it bears repeating: We all share the same fundamental wish for happiness. Every being wishes to be free from suffering. We must concern ourselves with the well-being of those people who are suffering because they are deprived of their basic human freedom. In an interdependent world, we are all responsible to change the external conditions.

When we see why we ourselves need freedom, we naturally wish our families to be free. The same reasoning can be extended to everyone else. We have a small family, related by blood or caregiving, and a big family, related by endless webs of connections. We can see the whole world as our bigger family. There is no one on this planet with whom we are totally unconnected. We have a connection to everyone, ultimately. Although our freedom struggle begins in the narrower scope of our own hearts and minds, it must reach its fruition in the broadest possible context of universal freedom.

EIGHT

Responsibility as Opportunity

OUR LIFE IS LIKE a vast net connecting us to all other lives on this planet, and each part of this net is linked to all of the rest. The essence of our life is not limited within the confines of our bodies but rather is distributed across all the people and things that we are connected to. To think about our life in a way that treats it as our individual property is too limited and too small, and leads us to miss seeing its full value.

When we assume that we are all separate persons, our responsibilities toward others are easily experienced as an encumbrance that limits our freedom. Just the language we use to speak of responsibilities—carrying, shouldering—suggests that we think of them as a kind of burden. Adopting the perspective of interdependence, however, can completely reorient our relationship to our responsibilities.

When we see that self and other are not separate and at odds but are part of an extended life that is shared, responsibility not only takes on a different meaning, it actually looks and feels different. When experienced from the standpoint of a consciously interdependent life, responsibility looks like opportunity. And it can feel a lot like love. As we expand our sense of ourselves, the meaning and feeling of responsibility expands too.

Others become the mirror in which we can see our own inner qualities reflected, and in that mirror we can find our own beauty reflected and enjoy it. Some people find it hard to see their own inner beauty. They wish to learn to be kinder to themselves but do not know how to go about doing so. I would say that in being loving and affectionate toward others, you can discover affection and kindness toward yourself. The best way to love oneself and care for oneself is to love others. The best way to exercise your individual rights and freedom is to use them to care for others—not because you feel obliged to but because of the basic truth of interdependence of all things and all beings.

Within whatever circumstances our lives are unfolding, we can each find ways to use our inner resources to fulfill the responsibilities we have toward one another as human beings. Responsibility is the opportunity to experience our connections in interdependence as love.

Speaking personally, the complex circumstances of my life as the Karmapa place various constraints on how I carry out my activities. We all have constraints of one sort or another. As I have mentioned, some of my constraints can prevent me from fulfilling the role of spiritual leader that I have trained for throughout my life. Had I dwelled on this perspective, I might have fallen into despair long ago. But then I meet people who come to see me. They share something about their lives, often their personal problems, and I try to offer some perspective that might be useful or inspiring. We connect, and sometimes I can observe their focus on their pain shifting a bit. They seem to gain some new strength and determination.

When this happens, it becomes clear to me that although my personal situation does have serious limitations, my life has value—not so much as something I live on my own but as something shared with and connected to others. This is an opportunity that responsibility offers.

We can all recognize that the planet cannot sustain our current rates of population growth. Seeing this, it might seem valid to say that each new human being born is an added burden to an already overburdened planet. To put it bluntly, we do not need more people on this planet. To push it even further, one might say that since the planet is already littered with human beings and the garbage we are constantly creating, one more person is just so much more garbage. This is a reasonable conclusion that we might reach if we were to adopt interdependence as our frame of analysis but apply it only in material terms. If each person is living solely for themselves, indeed it might be hard to see the value in having yet another person on the planet.

There is no denying that the environmental crisis we are facing today is greatly exacerbated by the dizzying rise in the number of human beings sharing this planet. This problem does urgently need to be addressed, but I do not think it can be solved by treating the value of human life in purely material terms or by seeing our lives as independent entities.

It depends entirely on our orientation. If we view a human life as distributed far beyond the limits of an individual's own body, we see that there are unique contributions that each person can make to the whole. Given the potential that each human being brings with them and can offer to all others, every human birth is something we are fully justified in celebrating, and every human life is to be cherished.

What's more, we can find the essence of our own being, and find the value of our precious human life, by looking past what is purely individual or personal and look to those we are connected to. When we treat ourselves as individuals disconnected from all else, the value of any one individual life can be hard to see. When we look at our life with a narrow and pessimistic view, we can feel discouraged about how little we can do. But we can broaden the scope of our awareness to include our connectedness to others—not only in material terms but also the connectedness of our inner qualities. It often doesn't take much to open up our angle of vision to see the great value of our lives. The opportunity to broaden our scope is always present.

If you stop to care for a single stray dog, one who is obviously distressed, frightened, and left to fend for itself alone on the streets, you can see the immeasurable value of your own life when you look into its eyes as you give him or her food or a scratch behind the ears. Every small action can be the turning point. It can be the stepping stone that allows you to see and reach beyond the narrow view that focuses on a separate self.

We should not judge the value of such an action solely from its immediate results. An individual act might actually be miniscule in terms of shifting others' external conditions, but its effect on the scope of our own awareness can be immense. As we learn to truly recognize how much the value of our life rests in our connectedness to other living beings, our relationship to our responsibilities can change dramatically. We will not want to miss any opportunities to deepen those connections and contribute to them positively. No action is too small to fundamentally reorient our life in this way.

Moreover, what our action means to the dog and what it means to us to engage in that caring exchange can have very little to do with the caloric intake of the meal or any other physical effect. The material exchange is important, of course, but its primary value is not material. The primary resources we are offering are inner resources—our love, protection, and care. They are received as comfort, security, and the easing of suffering. This is how others can serve as the mirror in which we see our own beauty.

When we encounter our own beauty—our value or worth—through our interconnectedness to others, we see something that cannot come to light when we are caught up in an ego-centered life. What we are seeing is the overwhelming value of interdependence.

What you find reflected around you can inspire you to embrace happily—in fact, eagerly and with joy—what you might otherwise see as duties or obligations. Responsibility becomes instead an important aspect of your personal value.

ACTING FROM LOVE

Living interdependence is the opportunity you have been waiting for. Perhaps the most valuable opportunity it offers is the opportunity to love. We need to expand our access to the love we have within us. This requires that we put ourselves in situations that ask us and allow us to love. I think love is like language. If we look at how language acquisition works, every human has the inherent capability to speak language. You could say we have the underlying design or infrastructure for human communication. However, if we do not have the conditions to learn a language, we will not develop that ability to speak, even if it is innate. If a human child is left in the wilderness and grows up there with no human contact, they may express themselves in grunts as animals do, but they will not be able to communicate in human language. We similarly have a natural capacity to love. But if we do not put ourselves in situations where it can develop, it will not grow to its full potential. That means we need an environment where at a minimum we hear the words *love* and *compassion*—even that can help.

Take ownership of your own love, by seeing it as something valuable that you have and can use. You can explore it, experiment with it, and enjoy it. You can even play with it, but most important is to practice extending it.

Numerous subtle mental factors create supportive inner conditions for love to grow, such as an intensity of feeling, a clear discernment, a vivid awareness, and so forth. No one of these alone is sufficient to make your love flourish fully. These elements all work together.

Enhancing the strength of any of them and keeping them in harmony helps your love thrive. This in turn transforms your relationship to your own responsibilities. The more you feel and act on love, the more you appreciate your responsibilities as opportunities.

GENEROSITY OF SPIRIT

Generosity can also help reorient our relationship to responsibility and sustain us in the lifelong process of fulfilling the responsibilities we all have toward others. Generosity is acting out of an attitude that has let go completely and does not hold on to anything for oneself. For our generosity to be perfect, we need not provide everyone with everything they need or want. It is not measured by whether we have singlehandedly ended poverty or world hunger. Since everyone has their own particular needs and particular circumstances, it is too much to ask that we could simply fill everyone's stomach and pocket, even if we had unlimited funds. Rather, generosity is primarily an attitude—a mental orientation—that manifests in the act of giving unstintingly whenever we have the chance.

Generosity need not be applied only in the material realm. We can also cultivate a spirit of generosity in whatever problem we are working on. We do this by making an offering of ourselves—offering a hand, offering a word, offering heart and mind—as a positive condition in any situation we find ourselves in. This attitude extends our open heart and mind into action and keeps us ready to act to benefit others.

When we are unable to accomplish grand plans or effect vast change, generosity also protects us against disappointment. Generosity of spirit helps keep our aspirations limitless, even when the results of our efforts are limited.

The Buddha is an example of someone who perfected the practice of generosity. What he did went far beyond giving away everything that came into his hands, although he did that too. He also ensured that his action was not limited to the mere act of giving. Inwardly, he offered to others the satisfaction and joy he himself received from giving, and he offered all the positive consequences of his act of giving to others as well. Even as he was giving a single thing that he happened to have to give at that moment, he reaffirmed his intention to additionally give whatever else he would receive in the future. In this way, he was continually projecting his generosity into the future. His actions were not limited to a single moment in time, to a single object or single being. Mentally, he was giving everything to all beings at all times.

Since the future is limitless and sentient beings are limitless, our aspirations can be limitless too. With this attitude, we can reach the end of any problem, because we can make our aspiration unlimited and project it as far into the future as needed until that problem is solved. This can make our resolve to extend ourselves as much as needed absolutely unwavering. When our aspirations are vast as the sky and extending until the time when all suffering is ended, we will not be disappointed or discouraged if we do not see the results immediately or even in a foreseeable future.

We hold nothing back—not our effort, not any resources that we have, not time itself. We do not even hold our futures to ourselves. If we limit our aspirations to short-term aims and allow our aspirations to end when we attain those limited results, we will not create the momentum needed to maintain our enthusiasm over the long haul, until that time when we have developed our qualities of mind and heart to their fullest capacity.

COLLECTIVE RESPONSIBILITY

We can use metaphors to help envision interconnectedness. I mentioned thinking of reality as a net. We can also see it as a fabric that has been woven through causal relationships. Like threads that run through a piece of fabric, the actions of one person serve as causes whose effects others must experience. In other words, the consequences of our actions can harm or benefit others. Responsibility is thus part of the fabric of reality. It is not an optional accessory.

There are different types of causality. One is the causality that we see at work in natural processes, such as the gradual emergence of a tree from a seed. There is also causality initiated by intentional actions on the part of humans or other sentient beings. What in Buddhism is called *karma* falls in this latter category. Some of the results of intentional actions rebound directly on the agent, but many of the consequences of our actions are experienced by others. The chains of events we set in motion are not purely neutral. We might benefit others, or we might harm them.

We are affecting others all the time. This is undeniable. This fact lies at the heart of our responsibility toward others as well as ourselves. Our actions might be beneficial or they might be harmful. When we stop resisting the basic reality that we do have responsibilities toward those whom our actions impact, we can begin to work with them, as opportunities to benefit others and to cultivate our own qualities, such as generosity, contentment, courage, and love.

What's more, when we join our aspirations and efforts with others, the effects we can have are far greater than what we can achieve as lone individuals. There is a great difference between sweeping with a single piece of straw and sweeping with a broom. If we join our straw with that of others, we can sweep away all that we wish.

Shared positive aims and aspirations are crucial for our collective actions to yield positive results. The effects of all our actions are shaped by the intentions that drive them. When we are united in our intentions, our actions have a much greater outcome. This is true whether the aspirations are positive or negative. Actions have amplified effects when performed collectively, and those effects can be beneficial or harmful.

The massive effects we have on one another can be seen clearly in something as apparently mundane as fashion trends. Everyone wants to wear the latest style, to look good in others' eyes and to feel good themselves. I have heard about what happened in the 1960s after Jackie Kennedy, the wife of the American president, had a leopard-skin coat made for her. Many people looked to her as a fashion icon, and when photographs of her wearing the leopard-skin coat appeared in magazines, she set a trend for wearing the skin of leopards and other spotted cats. By the time the fashion had moved on, a quarter of a million magnificent big cats had been hunted down and killed to meet the demand for coats made of their skin. In the collective quest to wear the latest style, people treated living, breathing beings as fashion accessories, causing them unthinkable pain and death.

When many other people join in a trend, we are less likely to look beyond the pack to think about the consequences of our collective actions, but actually we should think more. This becomes particularly acute in the twenty-first century, when technology further intensifies the reach of such collective actions. Imagine how many more animals would have been killed had the images of Jackie Kennedy in her coat been spread as widely as the Internet reaches in the globalized society of today. Seeing the fur on a screen can make it appear even more as an object for consumption and less as part of a being we might feel connected to and empathize with.

WITHOUT LIMITS

Many of the positive qualities and feelings we have been discussing—such as love, compassion, and responsibility—arise most readily toward those we already feel a connection to. Love surges in our heart when we see a beloved child or parent smile. Compassion activates strongly when we see a close friend or pet in pain. Love and compassion are integral to our interconnectedness, and it is our *feeling* of connectedness to the person or animal that allows us to experience love and compassion for them more strongly and spontaneously. But ultimately we are connected to all beings, as interdependence reveals. This means that even if we are not aware of or do not feel a particular connection to someone, the values of interdependence apply in our relationships to them. There is no real reason to extend them to some and not others. For this reason, just as equality must ultimately be applied universally, so must our compassion, love, and sense of responsibility. They must continue to expand until we willingly and enthusiastically embrace the opportunity to benefit any being with whom we come into contact. We include everyone, without exception—even the rich and powerful. In fact, there are important reasons for including those who are in positions of power among those for whom we feel responsible.

When we first encounter it, the idea that we should feel compassion or carry any responsibility for those with more resources than us may seem puzzling, and downright challenging. Whenever we are reluctant to assume responsibility for someone and feel it to be a heavy burden, this is generally a sign that our compassion is still too feeble or limited. As mentioned in chapter 6, someone is an appropriate object of our compassion because they suffer. No other reason is needed. As we deepen our understanding of what suffering is, we come to recognize that there is no one who does not suffer, and therefore there is no one who is not deserving of our compassion. The more compassion we feel, the more willing and able we are to accept our responsibilities toward others. Thus we have no basis for welcoming chances to help those afflicted by the conditions and experiences that we readily identify as forms of suffering—illness, hunger, poverty, physical abuse, discrimination—while we safely exclude those whom we consider well-off, because they have wealth and power. Although the materially prosperous may experience little physical discomfort, their unhappiness, distress, or painful mental and emotional experiences may exceed those with fewer economic resources. In other words, some may possibly suffer more. Being constantly driven by an insatiable thirst to acquire more is a deeply unsatisfying way to live. Competing to earn more, battling anxiety and fear of losing what one has already gained, constantly needing to have one's superior status affirmed, jealously guarding one's reputation—all these are miserable experiences that destroy one's peace and happiness.

Sometimes suffering is just a feeling we have when we are in a difficult situation. But we can be immersed in suffering even when we do not identify it as such. Just being under the control of disturbing emotions or subject to the destructive consequences of our own actions are forms of suffering. Our concern for others' well-being should not focus solely on the material conditions of their lives.

Since their main aspiration is to experience happiness and not suffer, as long as people still suffer inside, they are valid objects of our concern and responsibility. Moreover, since their suffering is internal, our own inner resources provide us abundant resources we can draw on to ease their pain and distress. This can strengthen our confidence to fulfill our responsibility toward others when they suffer.

Contributing to the authentic happiness and well-being of those who are better off than us is also pragmatic. The wealthy and powerful are in a position to impact large numbers of people. They may run businesses that hundreds or thousands depend on for their livelihood. They make decisions that therefore affect many people. If we truly want to care for the welfare of the impoverished or underprivileged, then surely we must also include in our concern those on whom the underprivileged are dependent and whose actions affect them. The motivations and conduct of the wealthy have far-reaching effects, and so by influencing them for the good, we can have a wholesome effect on many.

It is true that there are rich and powerful people who do not care for the general welfare and abrogate their responsibilities to society.

But that is itself a sign that they are afflicted by ignorance, greed, aversion, or other troubling emotions—and these emotions themselves are forms of suffering. Therefore we can feel compassion and directly or indirectly seek to do something to help them recognize the role they have to play and see their responsibilities as the wonderful opportunities that they are. Whatever we can do to help them come out from under their troubling emotions and use their role in society for good is a way to benefit them as well as others.

NOT THE SIZE OF THE CHECK

In a well-known scene in the Spiderman comics, Spiderman's uncle says to him as he lies dying, "With great power comes great responsibility." I am a fan of this superhero, but I would not put it this way. Certainly, having greater access to the world's resources—such as education, wealth, or mobility—gives you a greater ability to fulfill your responsibilities. But this is not the same as saying that having more resources to draw on means one is obligated to do more.

Rather, I think it is important to be fully aware and sensitive to the fact that the favorable conditions you enjoy means that you have greater ability and greater opportunity to make a positive difference in others' lives. This recognition can fire your enthusiasm to make the most of that opportunity to be a source of benefit to the world around you. You can feel that using your favorable conditions in this way is something truly worthwhile.

We should not be asking ourselves to give until it hurts, as an obligation. Rather, we should learn to truly feel that the value of our lives is greatly enhanced when we live our connections with and for others—as opportunities to connect with love and offer benefit. For this to happen, what needs to shift is not the size of the checks we force ourselves to write but our emotional relationship to responsibility. We do this by seeing responsibility as opportunity, grounding it in our most noble aspirations, approaching it with enthusiasm, and expressing it as a form of love that results in joy.

Reorienting our relationship to responsibility can lead us to seize and joyfully treasure opportunities to fulfill responsibilities. This means we will do more for others naturally. Such a change of heart motivates significant changes in our aspirations, and it results in sustainable and significant action.

I have many responsibilities as a spiritual leader. If I think of these as obligations, they can seem like a massive pile, one burden heaped on top of another, and I somehow have to shoulder them all. I could easily feel like a porter oppressed by a heavy load. Such an approach saps our joy and enthusiasm to meet our responsibilities and leaves us resistant or resentful when we think of all we must do and sacrifice for others. If you feel this way, rather than focusing on what you should do as an obligation, try seeing the conditions you enjoy as great opportunities that you want to seize and act on.

WE ARE ALL KARMAPAS

People have different capacities at different points in their own development. This is something to remember when we see others we feel are shirking their duties. It is also relevant in our own case. Just as we cannot simply order our mind to open instantly to its greatest extent possible, so too we must practice over time to see our responsibilities as opportunities.

To describe different phases of the spiritual path, Tibetan Buddhism speaks of greater and lesser vehicles with the idea that at different moments we are able to transport greater or lesser loads. Although broadly speaking, the Buddhist path is a path that anyone can follow, at the same time people pass through different stages of their development. We might begin our spiritual formation primarily motivated by a wish to free ourselves from suffering, at which point our spiritual practice, or "vehicle," is basically aimed at carrying one person forward: ourselves. But as we train to build up our spiritual capacities over time, the scope of the responsibility we are willing and able to assume expands. Eventually, we become both willing and able to carry everyone.

If we think in terms of our physical capacity, although we can train gradually to increase the weight that we can lift, ultimately we are limited by the material capacity of our body. But in the case of what we can carry mentally, there is no natural limit to what we can hold. We can slowly train to extend our capacity indefinitely. Our minds are not subject to the same limitations as matter. The mind has many untapped resources, and infinite agility. With mental or spiritual training, we initially learn how to be of true benefit to ourselves and from there gradually develop our ability to care for an increasing number of people until we encompass all beings.

I am a normal human being, but what is asked of me as the Karmapa is far beyond what can normally be expected of any human being. The title Karmapa means "one who performs the activities of a buddha." When I was young, I worked hard at my studies and by most standards did fairly well. Yet my teachers would say to me: "That's not bad. Pretty good. But you must fulfill the activities of a buddha in the world! You must do much better than that." Encouraging others to stretch past their current limits is fine and helpful, but that was taking it too far! The process should be gradual. Even if we see that others have the capacity to do more or be more, we cannot insist on them living up to their highest potential right from the outset.

From one perspective, my situation is unique. From another, it is not unique at all. I was given the grand title of Karmapa and informed from an early age that I had a responsibility to feel concern for everyone I came into contact with, and to benefit the whole world. There is nothing unique about having this responsibility; what is unique is that I was made aware of having it. We all share the same responsibility to care for others and be of benefit to the world. My title simply draws my attention to that fact clearly and means I had people reminding me of my responsibilities and encouraging me to develop the ability to fulfill them.

Now I would like to be one of the people reminding you that you have responsibilities to the world and encourage you to develop your own abilities to be of greater and greater benefit. It would be very strange if I were to declare that you are now the Karmapa. But that is how I feel. I often feel that everyone can and must be the Karmapa—a person who acts to benefit the whole world. We all have the same responsibility to do so.

For my part, I see having been recognized as the Karmapa as a precious opportunity to serve others and fulfill my responsibilities as a human being sharing this planet. Because of the specific conditions of your life, the opportunities that you will find to fulfill your responsibilities to the world will take different forms from the opportunities that I have. Nevertheless, we all have a precious human life and the precious faculty of human intelligence that allows us to discern what is harmful and what is beneficial. That alone gives us the opportunity to benefit a great number of sentient beings in a very vast way. If we really put this opportunity into practice, all of us will lead beautiful and meaningful lives.

What we can do is not fixed. We all have tremendous room within ourselves for growth. We can train ourselves to be able to benefit a larger number, more quickly, and with greater steadiness and skill. This is the idea behind learning to live our interconnectedness fully: We expand our concern and cultivate our capacity to act on that concern, until ultimately we are able to encompass the whole world in our concern.

With social and personal responsibilities, we tend to focus immediately on the loftiest responsibilities and expect ourselves or others to lift those right at the outset. This is impractical. Use your discernment to determine how much you can realistically carry, and then check that your expectations are not unreasonable. Do not be attached to lofty aims. Just start where you can. You can always grow from there.

LIVING THE CONNECTION

NINE

Sharing Resources

WE HAVE BEEN EXPLORING the inner qualities of inter-dependence that would allow us to live together more sustainably and compassionately on an interconnected planet. In order to direct our inner resources to that end, we will need to free ourselves of some deeply held views and habits. Central among these are the habits of comparing and competing, as well as the belief that supports them—the belief that competition is both natural and beneficial for our social and personal progress. No matter how deeply ingrained the habit to compare and compete is and no matter how natural it may seem, it is not our only option.

I have spoken of the twenty-first century as a century for sharing. Although the global society we have created may not favor this attitude, we now have a fuller context for understanding how counter-productive comparison and competition are in the greater scheme of things and a fuller awareness of the resources we can draw on to change them.

This can be as simple as shifting the basic paradigm we use in relating to others. When we treat ourselves as fundamentally independent and separate, we draw boundaries around ourselves that deny our fundamental and profound connectedness. Comparing and competing begins when we are separated in this way. We set our separate self next to other separate selves to see who stacks up better. We pit ourselves against others and work hard to increase the size of our own stack. We view the world's resources as something to amass and control. The concept of responsibility ends up looking like a tool to pry resources from those who currently have them. Being told we must assume responsibility and share our resources sounds like being told to give up our freedom. Protecting our freedom and protecting our resources come to amount to the same thing. It becomes very difficult to see any real reason to voluntarily share resources, unless it is to buy goodwill or some other personal advantage.

We fall into habits of quantifying everything and treat life like a zero-sum game in which others' gain will inevitably come at our loss. The most serious problems the world faces—from refugee crises to world hunger to environmental destruction—are greatly compounded when we respond with a reluctance to share resources. In the long run, such a response only brings negative consequences that we all suffer.

All this can shift when we shift our paradigm. When we start from the vantage point of interdependent individuals, rather than that of independent individuals, we can make our connectedness—rather than our separateness—the basis for all our interactions. When we act from an emotional awareness of that connectedness, the reorientation can transform not only our personal relationships but global society itself.

Our inner resources actually increase in the context of sharing and not in the absence of sharing. The one resource that we are all seeking, all the time—happiness—is unlimited, renewable, and most certainly increases when it is shared. When we truly and fully experience the truth of that fact, everything changes.

At present, the drive to compete is valued, encouraged, and practically required in our society. Many of our systems—economic and otherwise—operate in large part by stimulating and drawing on competitiveness between individuals as well as between companies and communities. Competition has yielded some important immediate results in the areas of survival and material development, but we should not let these advantages blind us to the serious disadvantages of competition.

Just look at how deeply we are harmed personally by our own habits of competition. Comparing ourselves to others is limitless. It has no natural end. In a life of competition, there is no final finish line we can cross so that we can rest and revel in our victory. There are always other people to compete against, and other races. In fact, one blends into the next so that life seems like one big race. This way of living has unintended but inevitable inner effects on us. When we live competitively, always reaching for more, we stimulate and strengthen a whole suite of inner conditions that disturb, trouble, and destroy our happiness—emotional states like resentment, jealousy, greed, and dissatisfaction. Greed is a hunger that only intensifies the more we feed it. The more we get, the more we want. If our life is based on competition and greed, our dissatisfaction will never end. We may have a functioning economy that harnesses competition and greed, but the one product this system never fails to produce is dissatisfaction—including for those who benefit from it materially. Building our society or personal lives on competition means we are building lives of guaranteed dissatisfaction.

This should give us serious pause. Setting our course in life by comparing and competing, we do not end up where we wanted to go. At best we end up where everyone else was heading—but they were just racing there because everyone else was too. When will we achieve the results we actually desire from all this toil and strife? Surely the goal we seek must include happiness, peace, and contentment. Have the supposed winners of this race achieved the goals of happiness and contentment? Or does the global consumer culture actually obstruct our pursuit of happiness?

If, upon careful reflection, we see that we are not closing in on the ultimate aim of all our striving, what sense does it make to continue an unrelenting competition that has no end and yields no reliable satisfaction? I believe our exploration of inner interdependence can help us take a more thoughtful approach to our lives and to the global society we are creating together.

We could measure our progress in life against our own inner standards and against clear values that we ourselves have consciously determined to be worth pursuing and upholding. This is a much healthier option than our present pattern of projecting our standard of measurement outside ourselves, and then judging ourselves relative to whomever we happen to find to compare ourselves to.

We already share a common aim of happiness and of freedom from suffering; this is the case no matter who we are, where we live, or how diverse the forms our personal quests take. This common goal forms a foundation for our universal equality. Until we have reached that goal, we are all valid objects of compassion and deserving of conditions that allow us to flourish. In a global society that extends those conditions only to those it calls "winners," and on top of that awards dissatisfaction to "winners" and "losers" alike, no one is actually winning. In fact, we have lost sight of the real finish line.

TAPPING INNER RESOURCES

The way we orient ourselves toward others profoundly impacts who we are and how we live. As we constantly compare ourselves to those above us in social hierarchies, we accept without question that it is best to have the latest, be the highest, and always rise to the top. In our jobs, for example, this tendency makes it important to stop and ask ourselves whether we really want to be promoted to a more senior position. Higher positions often leave less time to spend with family and friends and bring more stress that doesn't end when we leave the workplace. If we stop simply assuming that it is better to get ahead, we might recognize that we actually enjoy being more hands-on and having fewer administrative or managerial duties. We might not really need the increase in pay and might only use it to buy higher-status goods to go with our higher status. But much of the time we take the promotion simply because we think it means we are advancing. We have to have a strong inner clarity about our real priorities, and the resolve to protect them in the face of pressure to choose the higher rung on the ladder.

This same unthinking rush to upgrade is what fuels our consumer culture. For example, smartphones are everywhere. Everyone seems to have one and to want an even better one. The companies that produce them vie with each other to be the first to come out with new or improved features. The competition to make them more alluring is fierce. But for the consumers who have barely figured out how to use the features on their old phone, there should be no compelling reason to upgrade. However, when we hear the new version is coming out, we automatically feel we would like to buy it and are ready to throw away the perfectly good phone we already have.

If we feel the urge to compare, we are better off comparing ourselves with where we have come from, or with those behind or below us in these competitive schemes. We can train ourselves to stop comparing ourselves with those above and ahead of us and instead look back at the progress we have already made. This one simple shift we can make right now is a small measure to slow down our rush toward dissatisfaction.

Let's say the latest phone is an iPhone 6. As soon as iPhone 7—or whatever is next—comes out, that will be the best, and we will wish we could upgrade to that phone. It is certainly not the case that upgrading to iPhone 7 will fulfill any actual need, or somehow free up funds we could use for more beneficial purposes. The company is simply offering us a similar product with some mildly improved features and is basically counting on our faith that version 7 must be better than 6. When we compare version 6 to version 7, we feel dissatisfied with 6. But comparing it instead to 5 or even 4 can bring some contentment.

With a little reflection, we can recognize that the version we have now has more features than earlier versions—and more than we ever use, for that matter. We can be content and even delighted to have it, rather than feeling unfortunate not to have the latest model. Such a shift will allow us to make carefully considered decisions about when we need to upgrade and when we do not. More importantly, it enhances our happiness and frees us from the sense of lack we were looking to consumer goods to fill.

We can teach ourselves to feel basically satisfied not only with what we have but also with who we are. Many people feel they are not beautiful. It is not that they lack beauty; they simply have trouble seeing their own beauty. I heard of a study done where paintings were made of people based on their own verbal descriptions of themselves, and then a second painting was made of them based on descriptions by their loved ones. It turned out that the painting done based on the friends' description was much more beautiful. I think this is related to the climate of endless competition and comparison that is promoted by those who want to sell us what we feel we lack. People feel they are not beautiful enough and inadequate in all sorts of other ways. But these are ideas they have constructed themselves. If we could recognize instead the beauty that lies inside ourselves and in our connectedness, we would know that we already have all that we need, and more.

We face real challenges in reorienting ourselves and our society away from the habit of determining our worth by comparing. Consumerism itself is about comparing. The message that is consistently transmitted is: "This person has it, why don't you? You are falling behind. You should get it . . . now." Consumer culture takes hold within us and spreads throughout society because we are trying to measure up. We check whether we have risen to the level of others and figure out what to buy to maintain our status. Not only do we determine our worth by looking outside us in this way, but this habit inclines us to gauge personal worth in purely external and material terms. This devalues terribly the inner qualities that we so urgently need to draw on as our most important resources.

To counter this, we must cultivate our own inner standards—a clarity about where our true worth lies and a confidence in our own ability to gauge how we are doing in life. We need to determine for ourselves where the finish line is. As we do, we can also cultivate satisfaction, to encourage ourselves along as we recognize all the value we possess within us already.

Not only contentment but great determination and courage will be required to reorient ourselves. For even as we are pulled along by external, social forces, we are also pushed ahead by our own greed and dissatisfaction. The outer and inner conditions interact and reinforce each other. Even when we resolve to be less materialistic, social pressures lead us into old habits, sending us back to seek solace in social status and consumer goods. This makes it particularly hard to change direction. For this reason, we ourselves need to decisively free our minds. When we consciously ground ourselves in our own capacity for satisfaction and stay mindful of our real aim, we gain the traction we need to make lasting shifts, first in ourselves and eventually in our surrounding communities.

Our consumer lifestyle currently relies heavily on natural resources that are nonrenewable or take many millennia to be renewed. When we are asked to respond to that reality by reducing our consumption and finding new ways to share the earth's natural resources, people place their faith in science to come in and save the day. We trust that before fossil fuels run out, scientists will have found new means of extracting other energy sources from our natural environment. Many of us place our faith so completely in the power of science that we ask few or no questions about fracking or any new technique that is invented.

We expect science to save us from ourselves. We trust that new technologies will resolve any issues that arise as we perpetuate our existing way of life with escalating greed, consumption, and competition for resources and their devastating impact on the planet and other living beings.

When we observe how people in premodern times embraced religious views and blindly followed along with whatever religious authorities said and with whatever past generations had believed, we dismiss this as blind faith and superstition. I see much of the same nowadays when I look at how we display a similar trust in science and technology to solve the world's problems and give us a good life. Previously, people accepted answers from religious authorities without ever even asking the questions themselves and did not bother to analyze or seek to understand for themselves how things work. We do the same with science.

Actually, it seems to me that we are following science and technology with even more blind faith than the blind faith with which people used to follow religions. For all our sophistication, we seldom even ask which corporations and institutions are funding the scientific research and why, or what determines which of the proposed solutions are explored or implemented and why. These factors influence what gets presented to us, yet we imagine that science just reports the objective truth.

In the twenty-first century, religion's promise of eternal life in heaven has been supplanted by science and technology's promise of an eternally rising standard of living on earth. Our faith is so complete that we expect technology and science to defy even the basic law of causality. Collectively believing that science and technology have the power to protect us from the consequences of our own actions, we continue the same patterns of consumption and leave it to them to insulate us from the results.

Of course, it is not fair to place all the blame on today's scientists, any more than it was fair to place all the blame on religious leaders in premodern times. Many scientists themselves alert us to climate change, peak oil, species extinction, and many forms of environmental destruction. Clearly it is not scientists themselves, nor science and technology per se, that is the problem. The problem is our willingness to believe unquestioningly when we are told what we want to hear—that our way of life can last forever. We become susceptible to blind faith when we do not think deeply for ourselves, and we are especially inclined to believe in happy endings that we do not have to work to achieve.

If, despite the availability of sustainable energy sources that do not harm the earth, we ignore the environmental consequences and damage our collective home by continuing to extract more nonrenewable resources, that is just reckless.

Every single one of us has a part to play—consumers and suppliers, citizens, scientists, and policymakers. We can each apply our own intelligence by questioning the viability of the promise that our consumerist way of life can continue unchecked. The moment we recognize that our global consumption patterns are leading us in a dangerous direction, that is the moment to summon our courage, put on the brakes, and change course. This means reconsidering our way of life and significantly reducing our consumption.

Political candidates who challenge us to make serious changes to our way of life rarely even get on the ticket. They know such an unpopular stance can cost them the election. It is time to make this a more popular position. That is our duty. At a minimum we can express our skepticism when politicians tell us that science will keep the resources coming and that we can carry on as we are.

Scientists have a valuable part to play in analyzing the problem and creating options; corporate and political decision-makers can help make those options available. Consumers can contribute by utilizing the wiser options offered to them, even when those are not the easiest options. We consumers must make changes individually and also indicate clearly that we want and need change on a collective level. Every single person on this planet is a consumer. If consumers do not change, there is no one left to pass along the responsibility to.

This does involve modifying our individual patterns of behavior, which can be challenging. We are long accustomed to ease and convenience and are creative when it comes to finding excuses not to change. But if we are serious about protecting the planet's resources, it is indispensable that we find it in ourselves to change our feelings toward and our habits of consumption.

RESOURCES ARE LIMITED

As individual citizens sharing a global society, it is to our advantage—and is our responsibility—to educate ourselves about the reality on the ground. As interdependent individuals, we are not only affected by that reality, we are inseparable from it. The reality is that we are all dependent on one another and that everything is interconnected.

We, our country, other countries, and the whole world are all consuming as if natural resources will continue in an endless flow. But they have natural limits. We have looked at how things arise when the causes and conditions come together. By extension, when those causes and conditions are no longer together, things come to an end. Each cause and every single condition is likewise dependent in turn on its own set of causes and conditions. Eventually these chains of cause and effect circle the entire planet and leave out nothing. The web of interdependence links everyone and everything. This means when one thing changes, everything else eventually will also shift.

Those changes are often too subtle for us to notice, but they are happening all the time. Even though it is not immediately visible on a gross level, our nonrenewable resources are dwindling with every use. One day the natural resources we have been extracting from the earth will run out, and at that point our opportunity to do something about it will also run out. It will then be too late to moderate our consumption to make it consistent with the limits of the planet's natural resources. Our desire for the comfort that is driving our consumption of these resources has no natural limit. It must be self-imposed, and the time to limit our desires is now, not after it is too late.

Surely if we paused to think we would all recognize this. So why have we not done so as a society already? Part of the blame, I believe, lies in our failure to integrate an emotional awareness of interdependence into our way of living. When we do not feel ourselves to be connected to others, we do not act as if we were interconnected. We act instead as if our actions and their consequences were disconnected from others. And whether we are in the streets or at home, listening to what the media and marketing industry tell us, we are bombarded with the unrealistic promise that our lives can be lived in isolation from the consequences of our actions. It is as if we are prevented from considering these most basic truths—that actions have consequences and that things inevitably change. We need the space to step back and think for ourselves.

We urgently need to slow down, relax our minds, and think deeply about how we are living in an interdependent world. When we do, we can sincerely ask ourselves whether our attitudes and behavior are consistent with that reality or not. We can definitely find within us the infinitely shareable inner resources that we need. Unlike the external resources that we have such problems sharing, once we have a more realistic approach our internal resources can flow freely without limits, giving us the motivation we need to be able to share the limited external resources.

BUILDING A LONGER TABLE

Reflecting deeply on this issue is especially important for those in countries whose consumption of the world's resources is disproportionate to their numbers. Although it has only 5 percent of the world's population, the United States, for example, is estimated to consume 30 percent of the resources used annually worldwide.

For citizens of a powerful country, all the natural resources the nation controls can appear to exist solely for them alone. We must guard against an unexamined assumption that it is our birthright to consume as many resources as we can manage to acquire. The natural resources that we use were not created along with us and allocated to us alone at the moment of our birth.

The world's resources are a collective resource. They are not the private property of any one nation or corporation. As many environmental activists point out, they are not even the property of our generation. It is more accurate to see our natural resources as an inheritance that we are holding in trust for all the generations to come. We can see ourselves not as owners but as stewards treasuring and protecting this inheritance so that we can hand it on in the same or better condition as we received it ourselves.

At the moment, we behave as if we were basically alone in drawing on these resources. Wealthy nations hoard and waste, seemingly with-out concern for the fact that resources are dwindling for everyone. Leading the global competition to control resources, they may be able to defer the moment when their portion of the world's resources run out. But at some point they, too, will be among those who do not have enough—because there won't be any resources left, no matter how rich or powerful they are.

There is another way to view our advantages. When we observe that we have more than enough of something, this can instantly lead us to consider whether others might have an insufficient amount of it. We should not assume that everyone has the same opportunities and access to resources as us. Our having could well be coming at the expense of others.

In this same spirit, I recently heard a saying that if you have abun-dance, instead of building a higher fence, you might just build a lon-ger table. Having an excess can remind you that others are hungry or impoverished. It can inspire you to do something about that fact.

GLOBAL PRODUCTION OF INEQUALITY

Globalization seems to work on irreconcilable principles. It can function as a mechanism whereby powerful countries not only keep others away from their resources but even manage to secure their commercial and political interests outside their own borders. From a certain perspective, it can easily look as if the rich and powerful banded together to ensure the whole world developed in ways that they chose—and this development is very far from reflecting the fun-damental human equality that exists among all who share the world.

Multinational corporations seek out new markets to sell their prod-ucts for a good profit, and they also seek out poor countries where the costs to produce those goods are low. As we saw earlier, this means that factories and buildings can be made of substandard materials, and corners can be cut on safety and health measures, because people are poor and desperate enough to work for less than their labor might otherwise fetch in places where there are sufficient regulations in effect to protect their basic well-being. The "reasonable prices" that we pay for goods is the direct result of these conditions, and the whole system depends on and is designed to perpetuate inequality.

If we buy consumer goods, we are integral to these systems. Even if we grew all our own food and made all our own clothes, we would still be making use of the world's natural resources. There is no place on earth we can stand and validly say we are just innocent bystanders, uninvolved in any such dynamics. There is no place that interdependence does not reach.

WATER: A UNIVERSAL RESOURCE

Water is a resource so ubiquitous we might not imagine it to have limits. Water does not just sustain our lives. It is the very source of life on this planet. The possibility of human existence can be traced back to the presence of water. It evokes the very foundation of our inner equality, but access to it can vary greatly depending on our circumstances.

Living anywhere on the planet entails an intensive use of water. However, when we settle in arid zones, on top of the water we pipe in just to survive in that climate, we might take additional water to surround ourselves with lush gardens and green lawns. Sprinklers run to grow grass in arid but affluent corners of the planet, while people who do not even live in a desert are desperately thirsting for the same clean water we are spilling elsewhere without a second thought. People who newly arrive in such neighborhoods and observe the lifestyle would never believe that they were in a desert.

Those of us who live in communities with ample material resources can go through much of our lives without recalling that elsewhere people are dying for lack of clean drinking water. The same attitude we see on the level of individuals happens between nations. We act as if having easy access to something entitles us to squander it if we wish.

We let differences in our circumstances blind us to the utter sameness of our needs. This is why it is so important to learn to draw on inner resources, to feel connected to others who share the same basic needs but happen not to be living amid the abundance we enjoy. Just because we can simply push a button or turn on a faucet does not mean the resources we are tapping are ours alone to use—or waste. Having access to natural resources does not imply entitlement to treat them as our own exclusive inheritance.

The resources of the earth are our common wealth. There is absolutely no basis for thinking that the earth's water belongs to some people more than others. Our thirst is felt equally, and our bodies depend equally on clean drinking water. The water we have belongs to all species on this planet.

By widening awareness of interdependence, residents of arid zones can take their environment as a reminder of how precious each drop of water is. They can inspire themselves to take extra care in their use of water, from turning off the water when brushing their teeth to rethinking which plants they cultivate in their gardens.

LIVING BREATHING PLANET

Scientists tell us that our forests are disappearing at a terrifying rate, fossil fuels are running out, and the tiny percentage of the earth's water that is drinkable is diminishing. We know all that, but clearly intellectual knowledge alone is not effecting enough change in our behavior. We need to learn to feel how very precious and rare our resources are, to shift from mind to heart.

Perhaps it would be better to think of our natural resources not as substances or things but as living beings. Thinking this way allows us to feel the personal connection that is already in effect. We have a relationship to the planet and all its abundant resources, a relationship through which we receive but through which we give as well. Some native Americans and other indigenous peoples see water and mountains as animate beings—as sacred. When we see the earth's resources in this way, we can feel that we are connected to them personally. This can move us to respect them and wish to care for them. I think this sense of having a living relationship with the earth's resources is necessary for us to change the way we relate to them and treat them.

Sometimes people who know of my interest in environmental protection ask me whether trees and other living things can be included as objects of our compassion. What I personally think is that even if they do not have an actual feeling of suffering, they clearly do yearn to survive. Trees take such a long time to grow, seeking out all the nutrients and sunlight they need, adapting to overcome adverse conditions. We can see plants sprouting up in the most inhospitable places—from cracks in rocks and between the cement slabs of sidewalks. They seek out the favorable conditions they need and avoid those that harm them. We can see them protecting themselves. This indicates that plants yearn to flourish. We cannot exactly say that they *want* to survive, but there is no denying that all living things display a drive to live. I think we need to respect that.

The yearning to live is something we share with them. Recognizing that shared drive could lead us to behave very differently when we make use of the planet's forests and other living things. I have no doubt that if human beings acted with emotional awareness of plants' yearning to live, life on our earth would be a great deal healthier.

SCALING UP

Once we feel a personal responsibility to steward the world's living resources, the next question is how we can change course and live more compassionately and sustainably on this planet. The challenge is admittedly huge, because so much is already in place to keep us running together mindlessly in the same reckless direction. However, precisely because of interdependence, the future is being created by the causes and conditions we generate today. If we change our conduct today, we are already changing the future.

I spoke of limiting our personal consumption, but sometimes people tell me that they feel that anything they could do would be a mere drop in a huge ocean and would be too little, too late. We need to be brutally honest with ourselves and consider whether our belief that we personally cannot have any real impact is just an excuse to avoid changing our own habits.

Waiting for someone else to take the first step just leaves us stuck in the same place. Delegating the task completely to those in power does not work either. Leaving it to a few people in key leadership positions to take up the cause is not a realistic way to enact change, because this is not how interdependence operates. Even the most powerful agent for change always brings about change in conjunction with others. When an influential person does decide to make a difference, that decision will have had its own causes and conditions that others may have worked to create. A leader's decision might be the result of some people educating them about the problem and others inspiring them to be a force for change. Hearing of a project that the local community implemented, or reading of the suffering that environmental negligence caused for the children of another community might be the decisive condition that leads them to take up a cause.

Once people in key positions do decide to act, they will also need backing. Even the thickest straw in the broom is strengthened immeasurably by being joined with others. Political leaders may need support to counter the powerful interests that their party serves. They will need to point to something to show others that there is a movement for change that cannot be denied. Your vote and your local project could be that something.

Each and every one of us bears a responsibility, and has an opportunity, to bring about the needed changes—to identify them, to inspire them, and to implement them. We each have different opportunities to contribute to change based on our circumstances and our particular position within the chains of causality that are leading to the problem.

One role that we all play is as consumers. Who are these energy sources being extracted from the earth for? For us, the consumers. If we want change, we need to raise public awareness, and we have to ask for it together, sending a clear and consistent message. As we saw in discussing responsibility in the last chapter, collective action has amplified effects.

We need to express collectively what we want and need, through our actions as well as our words. As it is, with our actions of consumption, we are already sending one message, expressing what we want and what we are willing to pay for it, environmentally as well as economically. If we really want producers to recognize that we want and need something else, our actions have to become consistent with our words. Our personal consumption has to be part of the way we communicate our appeal for change. In fact, because of the close interdependence between producers and consumers, if we consumers change our behavior, producers will invariably change as well.

Just as we depend on them, so too they depend on us. This two-way relationship itself puts change within our reach. Being connected means we change one another. Throughout this book, we have been discussing how change is not only possible but inevitable and discovering how we can direct that change in positive, productive ways. Our inner resources are powerful forces for initiating and implementing change. Habits can be reshaped. Our discernment and our empathy, our compassion and our generosity, and our sense of responsibility and contentment can all be made to work together. We can draw on these and our other interdependent inner qualities to shift to productive, sustainable practices that end our current cycles of harm—harming other people, animals, and the natural world.

Finding a way of life that is truly sustainable entails not only shifting from nonrenewable to renewable material resources, but also making greater use of our inner resources, which are all themselves renewable. We can each become scientists, experimenting within ourselves to find the right conditions for our inner resources to grow stronger and remain stable and accessible, so that we can bring them to the world.

When we place our interconnectedness at the center of our life, empathy and contentment can become the primary resources that we turn to first. Instead of greed, we base our lives in contentment and moderation. Instead of competition, we make sharing and compassion the basis for our interactions. These shifts are not idealistic. They are in fact shifts to an approach that is far more pragmatic. It is not pragmatic to hope that the world's resources can meet the demands of our unbounded greed. But if we approach the world's supply of raw goods with a spirit of sharing and a sense of contentment that *can* appreciate what we do have, the earth's limited external resources would be matched by the appropriate inner attitudes. That is an approach based in reality.

Turning away from competition and comparison and toward the connections of interdependence can be a conscious act of resistance. It can form part of our personal struggle for freedom, in which we liberate ourselves from the inner forces of greed and dissatisfaction that leave us vulnerable to manipulation. This gives us the freedom to consciously embrace opportunities to share.

We can be different and we can be equals, sharing our existing resources and creating shared beauty. When we bring inner resources like contentment or compassion together with the world's outer resources, we will have a truly sustainable planet. We need never exhaust the bounty that we already have gained just by being born as humans on this interdependent earth.

TEN

The Value of Community

HUMAN BEINGS are profoundly shaped by the communities in which we participate. Before we join any particular community, we are already part of the human community. Each of us is far more deeply marked by being human than we are by our membership in any other community—even as formative and intimate a community as our own family. Likewise, the basic responsibility we have as human beings holds priority over any claims made on us by any smaller or more local community.

Before anything else, I feel we should identify ourselves first as human beings. Many of the unhealthiest dynamics in society arise because we fail to honor the primacy of our membership in the community of humanity. When identifying with particular communities—family, religious, ethnic, national, or otherwise—we need to guard against even subtle contempt, resentment, or aversion for those outside that community. At the same time, whatever values or qualities we cultivate in the context of our more limited communities, we must ensure that this is done in the service of shared human values.

Our particular identities need to be compatible with our human identity. This does not mean we all have to be the same. It means that each particular community should be oriented toward making a contribution to the whole and should not detract from or demean other communities.

In my own case, I have been part of a Buddhist community my whole life. I was born to a close-knit Buddhist family. My parents had little education in Buddhist doctrine but great devotion to the basic values taught in Buddhism. Everything in our surroundings was Buddhist, and my parents' faith was unswerving. On top of that I was recognized as the Karmapa as a young boy and have been fully immersed in Buddhist culture and traditions since then. Who would dare argue that the Karmapa is not Buddhist? If asked whether I am Buddhist, I do not even get a split second to consider my reply, since there is only one answer. You can hardly get more Buddhist than the Karmapa! But before we worry about how we are doing in terms of our religious, ethnic, or other local identities, I think we need to ask ourselves how we are doing as human beings.

For me the answer is not so automatic. I ask myself sometimes how I am doing as a human being—whether I am a good human being—and sometimes I think I am not too bad, but sometimes I feel I am falling very short of the mark. I am not nearly so sure that I am fulfilling my responsibilities as a member of the human community well. But if I am not a good human being, what am I doing as a Buddhist?

Keeping in sight the full human community can help us avoid the division into "us" and "them" that causes so much harm in society. Maintaining a vivid awareness of the fundamental equality of all humans allows us to actively welcome difference. It lets us see our diversity as enriching us all rather than as dividing us into antagonistic factions. We need communities that value universal human equality—not those that assert kinship among its members while fostering enmity and denigration for those outside it. Especially when our segment of society enjoys advantages not open to others, we need to be very careful that our sense of ourselves as members of that privileged community does not make us feel entitled to overlook our shared humanity with those outside our circle.

Social problems arise when we accept equality, inclusiveness, or compassion merely as abstract principles and do not apply them in our day-to-day interactions. There is little benefit in principles that we only work with in our heads and not in our interactions with real people. That is why learning to live our interdependence and equality on the level of our particular relationships and communities is key. We have to start with what we experience toward specific human beings, bringing forth the real and vivid feeling of our intimate connections and gradually working to expand that sense of connectedness to others. Since the inner qualities necessary for this expansion are infinitely renewable, we can approach this with the confidence that the intensity of our sense of connectedness need not diminish as it expands. There is no natural limit to our feelings of interconnection.

Community is of tremendous importance to our personal flourishing. It can bring profound meaning to our lives. However, if our participation in a particular community shapes us in a way that is inconsistent with or not supportive of our more fundamental humanity, we will not grow well. Only when the activities of our local communities—or the advice and practices of the religious community we belong to—clearly recognize our basic responsibility and worth as human beings and hold to our human values will we truly gain positive results from being part of those communities. When we do keep our basic humanity in clear view, our community engagement will help us to become better people. Our attitudes, our conduct, and our lives will improve, and that positive growth will contribute to the flourishing of the human community as a whole.

NO PLACE OUTSIDE COMMUNITY

To say that we are humans independently of any particular community affiliation is by no means to say that we are fundamentally independent of any community. People can opt to give up their membership in some communities. They move out of old neighborhoods, change religions, or lose touch with groups of friends. People might even fall out with their birth families and seek to reject and disown them. However, whether or not you can truly separate yourself from such communities, you can never leave the human community.

Even if we shun society and live alone in a log cabin or a cave, we are still benefiting from human knowledge about how to survive in nature. In order to find food, make shelters, and stay warm, we are using information and technologies that were transmitted to us as a member of the human community. Conversely, our stay in the wilderness can have a profound impact on society itself. What we learn there might greatly enrich humanity. Both Buddha and Jesus spent time alone in the wilderness. Many others' apparent shunning of human society has had far-reaching impact, such as the American naturalist Henry David Thoreau or the Tibetan yogi Milarepa. Far from being irrelevant, those who withdraw from social contact can even start movements that dramatically change society as a whole or inspire people across generations to rethink their priorities.

AVOIDING EXCLUSIVE ENTITLEMENTS

I have mentioned that others can be mirrors in which we better view ourselves. As we care for others and extend ourselves to them, we can see the beauty of our own positive qualities in them. The world itself is a big mirror for us. In that largest of mirrors, the part we occupy will appear tiny amid everything else. We will hardly be able to see ourself, and we may appear insignificant. However, if we look into a smaller mirror, we and our connections to others will appear prominently and clearly. In that smaller mirror, we see that we have a place. That mirror is community.

Whatever we do in our personal life becomes part of what society is doing and helps shape it. We need not join any particular association or community to impact society. Our individual actions contribute to collective action whether we intend it or not. Although the people working in a single company or a single industry may differ in many ways, they also hold a great deal in common. The same is true of people living within the same society. Even without explicitly joining forces or coordinating our efforts, when many people act in similar ways and have similar intentions, their actions have a cumulative and collective effect.

Let's say you normally take care to put your trash into a waste bin, but you are out for a walk and do not see anywhere to put your garbage. So you throw a tissue or candy wrapper on the ground. This appears to be an isolated personal act, one single piece of litter. You may feel, "I usually put my garbage in the trash bin, so just this once does not count." But a pile of garbage is nothing more than the accumulation of various pieces of litter discarded by individuals with a similar attitude. One person's act of littering serves as a condition for others to litter, as they see your garbage lying around and have the sense that littering is acceptable in that area.

You may also see other people's garbage and think, "I am not really a litterer, and it is not my job to clean up the garbage." So you walk on. This is precisely how we end up having a collective problem with trash. Our individual actions have effects that are shared, whether or not we consciously sought those effects and whether or not we are aware of them. Individual actions create and reinforce social patterns.

There is a kind of wry joke that is made about the garbage in India. Actually, it is not really a joke so much as a sad observation.

Cows often eat the garbage that is lying in the street, which includes many cardboard boxes and plastic bags. Some people quip that this progression from fresh grass to cardboard boxes and plastic is a sign that the cows are more modern! Many cardboard boxes have staples in them, and the cows eat these along with the cardboard, and the harm is quickly compounded.

The task of collecting garbage in India used to fall to specific communities of outcastes, and people of higher castes would not stoop to touch garbage. Nowadays in India and throughout the world, we leave that job to the sanitation workers. We feel we can walk past garbage on the street, since we do not belong to the garbage-collecting caste or waste-management profession. In some parts of the world, not only do people feel that they have no duty to pick up trash, they feel they are among those entitled to throw it on the ground. In other places, littering is no longer considered socially acceptable, and so people do not openly litter. However, we can see trash on sidewalks and roadsides all over the world, and when we see litter on the ground, we are looking at the sign that someone did not feel responsible for cleaning up after themselves.

This same attitude of entitlement is reflected in many wealthy nations, where it is considered perfectly acceptable to relegate the most menial, disagreeable work to others—often immigrants or disempowered minority communities—as if our social responsibilities could be outsourced. The division of labor in society should not blind us to the responsibilities to society that we all share simply by virtue of being human. If we are not careful, our sense of belonging to one community rather than another can lead us to feel that particular— usually, disagreeable—responsibilities are beneath our dignity and belong instead to others of a different social class. This happens precisely when our identification as members of particular communities gives us a sense of entitlement to rights and privileges that we do not wish or plan to share universally.

Different communities can and do have different contributions to make. This diversity is necessary and valuable. But each community must take care that its particular contributions enhance the human community as a whole and do not harm or exploit other communities. We can accomplish this by keeping vivid within us a recognition of our basic value and responsibilities as a human being, rather than waiting for some subgroup or other to step in and clean up the messes we have made together.

OUR FIRST TRAINING GROUND

As I have said, I was born to a nomad family, and when I was young our family came together every night in our large shared tent. At that altitude, the temperature drops greatly once the sun goes down, and my parents would make a fire in the center of the tent. We would eat our stew together in the evenings, and the older members of the family would tell stories. I was very young then and remember my mother would give me a bowl of the fresh milk of a dri—the female counterpart to the male yaks. Dri milk is very rich, and invariably I would nod off as I sat in the warm glow of that fire. That milk was really the best sleeping medicine. I slept on a bed of stones that had been piled up for me. When I look back on it now, I really cannot imagine how I could sleep on those slabs of rock, but I did sleep there very cozily.

This was my first experience of community—the community of family—and it was my first lesson in the value of interdependence. I witnessed this rhythm day after day, sharing very simple things of life—simple food, a warm fire, and most of all, enjoying each other's company. Hearing the tones of each other's voice, we could find a deep contentment. We were able to feel happy for all that we had, even though in terms of material things we had very little.

Whether we were laughing or upset, those experiences were shared. If one family member fell ill, we were all concerned. We learned in a perfectly effortless way to care for one another. No one needed to explain to us that we were profoundly interconnected. Our family life and community life can be our first teacher of this most fundamental reality that we are part of each other and not separate. Whether we learn this in our family or in other communities, it is an indispensable life lesson. For a healthy global society, we must internalize this basic fact that we each contribute our own part to the whole, and that we must therefore look after each part in order to create a world that is complete and flourishing.

It is simply not enough to engage with interdependence through empirical evidence, observable data, and abstract theory. For our awareness of interdependence to be of benefit, we must go well beyond that. Interdependence is a reality that we urgently need to learn to feel, and a healthy community can help teach us how to cultivate the emotions that enable us to flourish in that reality.

In a close-knit family, you naturally feel that you are surrounded by the moral support that makes difficult times bearable. Your suffering is lessened because you feel it is shared. At the same time, when you share in the happiness of a community of ten people, you do not get just one tenth of a portion of happiness. Rather, each person gets a full and complete share of happiness. This may defy mathematics, but it makes emotional sense. It makes sense precisely because we are not the discrete units that the autonomous model of individuals tells us we are.

I realize that modern families do not generally sit around the fire together in the evenings like mine did. Many are as likely to read words on a screen as they are to hear them from the mouths of their family members, and some stay abreast of each other's lives via Facebook or Instagram. Families face all the same issues in connecting directly that we explored in chapter 2. In our era of connectivity, it might be wise to make a practice of consciously turning off the screens, so we can allow closeness to blossom slowly and directly. It is especially important to give time and attention to the form of community we are creating in our family, because whether done intentionally or not, this is where we develop important habits of relating to our own interdependence with others.

In the best of circumstances, parents are the first sources of encouragement and the first guides in developing our inner resources. When this training is encouraged from childhood, we have easy access to the innate compassion and openness that can be obscured later in life. But even as adults, we can take the natural human experience of close interconnectedness and extend it from our smallest community outward in stages. We can consciously apply it to other local communities we feel part of, and from there to larger community.

In this way, with time and patience, we make it a practice to widen our sense of family. This entails recognizing that we are related to others in endless ways. Most importantly, it means allowing the sense of sharing and the feeling of connectedness to reach those beyond our biological or chosen family. Ultimately, we seek to extend that sense of closeness to the entire human community.

In our immediate communities of family and friendship we naturally feel the reality of interdependence without any need to refer to abstract principles. The same truth of interdependence is operative in the smallest of interpersonal scales—between ourselves and those who nurtured us directly—and on a global scale—our connections to all human beings, or even all living beings. We need to take the natural feeling for interdependence that we gain in the smallest scale and broaden our perspective to be more and more inclusive, until it includes all living things.

TRAINING TO LIVE INTERDEPENDENTLY

Communities also offer especially fertile ground for two other key aspects of the training in living interdependence: developing awareness and engaging in action. We have already seen the amplified effects our actions have when they are enacted in concert with others as collective action. Participating actively in a local community can help us break out from seeing ourselves as isolated individuals, powerless to change the world.

Sharing in the responsibility for bringing about well-being in a smaller community can allow us to gain confidence in our ability to make a positive impact on a broader scale. A large-scale community such as global society may seem abstract and theoretical. But within a smaller community, you can experience tangible positive effects of your contribution. You can see that your goal is reachable, step by step. You see that you were able to bring about one part of that larger goal.

Local communities are like what you see when you zoom in on an image. If you are looking at the whole globe, it is hard to imagine you are making any difference. But if you zoom in closely, to your family and friendships, you can see that your presence is important. You are having an impact. From there you can zoom out a bit. After the tightest focus on your family, the next scale where you can see your impact is your surrounding community. Just as you can see how much you can impact and really change in the family, you can also see it in other small communities you form part of, such as your classroom or workplace. The key point is to recognize that you are having the same impact all the time. The only thing that changed was the setting of your lens. Focusing first on the impact you have in your smallest and most local communities allows you to gather confidence as you scale up to act as a member of the global human community.

You can make good use of technology to do this exercise. I did something similar once with Google Earth. After locating the area of Tibet where I lived with my family as a boy, I traced the rivers and valleys where all the events of our family life took place. All the days caring for each other were spent there, and all the evenings coming together around the fire. It might look smaller as you zoom out, but this is an illusion. The size has not changed. You just lost sight of it in the larger frame. You can zoom back in and the world in which you make a difference is still there. The impact you make is not lost.

COURAGE BUILDS INCLUSIVE COMMUNITIES

When we fail to create a place for everyone in our communities, we reinforce the patterns of *us* and *them* that are at odds with the reality of interdependence. This blinds us to our root equality and leads us to push many people to the margins of society, such as the sick, depressed, and old. This is a failure of courage. It is fear that makes us shun the sick, and we likewise shun those who are different from us—old people with their different ideas and ways and so on. Compassion needs to be accompanied by courage in order to come to its full force in the world. The courage and confidence we gain in our smaller communities helps us expand our sense of community until it embraces the whole human community.

It is most often the weak and vulnerable—human and animal alike—who are shunned from communities, often in horrific and painful ways. In ancient times in Tibet, people suffering from leprosy were treated in such a way. When someone contracted leprosy, they were chased away from their homes and their villages like stray dogs. There was no cure for leprosy, and people thought it was highly contagious, and so those afflicted with it were shunned completely. Today it might be the homeless, the poor, the aged, or the diseased to whom we turn a blind eye, or worse.

Extending community to include those who are lonely or left out is a training in compassion. Those who are shunned are particularly vulnerable and need exceptionally strong compassion from us. We should not allow ourselves to limit our compassion to feeling pity, hoping their sad situation goes away. This sort of pity may look like compassion, but it is fundamentally selfish, since we preserve a comfortable distance between ourselves and those who are sick or troublesome or whose views do not match our own. This "compassion" may make us feel better and improve our image in our own mind, but it does not actually help anyone.

To me, the annual slaughter of livestock among nomads in Tibet is another example of this. We Tibetan Buddhists speak of wanting to free all beings from suffering, but we are effectively saying to the animals, "I have compassion for you, but now I need to kill you." We really cannot have it both ways, claiming a heart of compassion while our body is busy enacting the suffering of others. It is not always easy to bring our attitude and conduct into alignment, but it is always possible.

Compassion is not something to keep locked inside yourself. It is something to express in action. This compassion must persist beyond the thought, "If only their suffering would come to an end." If we focus too long on wishing for something that we never pursue and that never happens, we run the risk of falling into a depression ourselves. When compassion arises, it is the time to act.

When our compassion is not anchored in courage and a firm commitment to act effectively, we cannot even see those in society who suffer most and therefore warrant the most compassion. Courage gives us the force to face any challenge and lift any load that needs lifting. It also transforms our wish for something to happen into a promise to do it ourselves. When there is courage, compassion can become a promise that we know we will deliver.

KEEPING VIRTUAL COMMUNITIES REAL

Social media have opened many new possibilities for forming and connecting communities. Yet the shift toward virtual communities means our connections are increasingly mediated by technology. Our online connections have an unreal quality to them, like dreams. As we saw in chapter 2, our relationships become more shallow when they are so heavily mediated by electronic connections.

We create false online personas and behave in ways we would not do with people we actually saw and heard. We ourselves can end up captivated by our electronic selves. We invite people to interact with that virtual image we have created and carry out more and more of our relationships online. In the complete absence of direct sensory contact, it can be unclear whether we are connecting to a person or to a machine—or to a fantasy.

I am skeptical that virtual communities can fulfill the function of a real community. Certainly there are some positive aspects of online communities, but many of them are fundamentally commercial in nature. If nothing else, this means that they have other aims beside a purely altruistic wish to foster healthy and compassionate communities. Of course, not all online communities are created to turn a profit for their founders, but once a community forms, the temptation is there to use those connections to generate revenue or promote self-interested agendas.

I've even heard that in Japan nowadays, people are so starved for direct personal connection that, if you want someone to talk to and spend time with, you can rent a friend. Just book their time, and they will come be your friend for a few hours or a few days. This really makes me wonder about the future.

Though we may be becoming too reliant on technology, investing it with too much blind faith, technology does provide us with much that is of benefit. Some years ago, a trip I had been planning was cancelled at the last moment. This was disappointing to many people, myself included. But the technology had just been put in place where I lived, in northern India, to transmit a live talk online. There continue to be many more places and far more friends than is possible for me to visit, and that became the first of what is now a standard practice of webcasting talks live. At the time of that very first webcast, I had the thought that although my body had not been able to make that trip, I could send my voice and my mind and heart over the Internet to the people I had wanted to visit. Whatever the challenges and pitfalls, technology does offer important ways to maintain a community's connections even when there is physical distance among members.

The Internet works because many people are connecting and making distinct contributions that are distributed around the vast network. It works because of interdependence. Whenever we log on to check our email or to search for information, we may feel that we are alone in front of our screen. But in fact we are connecting to numberless other people, each in front of a screen like we are. With some creativity, we can make good use of our time online by using it to strengthen our awareness of interdependence. You could try pausing each time you are about to go online. You do not need to do anything; just pause to notice and *feel* that you are about to be connected with millions of people around the world. Allow yourself to acknowledge their presence at some other node in the vast shared network, wherever they are, and feel your connection to them.

Once you connect, you can find abundant opportunities to use the Internet to cultivate compassion. Everywhere online you find descriptions of tragic situations around the planet. Even if you do not know the people involved personally or have any direct connection to them, you can allow yourself to feel their need for happiness or freedom, or anything else that they lack. You can open your heart to that. Since you know that you share with them the same basic wish to be happy and to be free of suffering, and the same basic human potential, you already have a connection to them. On that basis, you can strengthen your determination to seek ways to send them care, love, or any other resources they lack.

These are some ways to mitigate the depersonalizing effect of relating to others electronically. But as I have said earlier, the human warmth that is transmitted when you can see and hear one another and interact directly has a value that cannot be reproduced by cables and circuits. Communications technology breaks our friendships into bits of data, bounces them off satellites, and scatters them around. When we want to reach out to connect with a real, living person, there is literally no one there. Infusing our contact with others with the vividness of direct perceptions is important not only for building community. Sensory contact is key in ensuring that compassion and other qualities of interdependence make the transition from principle to action in the world. The suffering of others does not exist as mere images in our brains or on an electronic screen, so our compassion cannot simply take place in our heads. It needs to make the transition from head into our heart, and from there flow out through all our senses and all our pores so that we are connecting and living that connectedness fully. Our compassion must not stay trapped inside us. It must move us to action that has a real impact.

BUILDING AN INNERNET

Initially the Internet linked only a limited number of computers. You could say it started as a small community. Developers learned how to create stable connections that could stay open and facilitate exchanges among all parties. From there it extended gradually, opening to include more and more people. We could do something similar in forming communities that are consciously founded in our shared interdependence. For that to work, our smaller networks have to have expandability built into them. They cannot be founded in exclusion. This is why it is so important to build our smaller communities in a way that reflects and respects the larger human community of which it is a part.

I think along with the Internet, we should develop an *Inner*net. A number of techniques from the traditional Buddhist training can help us do so, by cultivating a universal sense of connectedness. Although these methods are widely practiced in Tibetan Buddhism, one certainly need not be Buddhist to use them. Several of them start with existing connections that readily evoke an authentic and immediate sense of concern and then expand from there.

For many people, the relationship to their mother is such a relationship where warm feelings arise spontaneously. The mother is not the only example of this, of course, nor does it work for everyone. We can also do this on the basis of any other close relative—a father, grandparent, sibling, friend, or even a pet. Whoever it is that we feel the most affection and tenderness for, we gradually train ourselves to feel toward all other beings the same warmth and concern.

But for many people the mother serves as a good starting point, since all the fullness of sensory contact is vividly present in our earliest interactions with our mother. She bore us and in most cases cared for us when we were small, holding us, caressing us, and feeding us. Very often our mother protected us when we were defenseless early in life. The compassion of a mother is a courageous, active form of compassion. One of the Buddhist techniques for consciously cultivating compassion encourages us to feel that each person is a mother to us. This allows us to extend the community that links us to our mother to encompass others as well.

In Tibetan Buddhism, we generally do this by reflecting that in some lifetime or another, each person has been our mother and cared for us and protected us in that life with great tenderness. This, of course, works best for those who believe in past and future rebirths. There are ways it can be adapted for those who do not share those assumptions, but first it may be useful to present the Buddhist reasoning.

In the Buddhist viewpoint, we note that although it is difficult to prove that our consciousness had other lives before this one, it is just as difficult to prove that our consciousness began in this lifetime. Even answering the question of when matter first began is difficult.

When we contemplate the origin of the universe, if we ask when matter first appeared or how it was created, science is effectively unable to posit any sound answer. In the case of mind or consciousness, a beginning point is even more difficult to posit. Since everything that arises must arise from causes and conditions, we cannot say consciousness appeared randomly out of nowhere. We also cannot say it arises from the brain, since the brain is matter and consciousness is not. Therefore in Buddhism we posit a continuity of consciousness that has been taking different forms of birth since beginningless time. We infer that in each and every one of those births, we were connected to a set of parents. For that reason, we can say that every single other being in principle could have been our parents in one of those numberless past lives we have led.

However, for many people this idea of rebirth is not comfortable or convincing. One need not accept past and future lives to develop a strong family feeling toward all beings. We can also construct it gradually through other means. Giving us food and clothes is one way our parents care for us when we are small. We now have other people who do that for us and also offer us many forms of support and protection. We can readily see that they benefit us like parents.

I myself was born to very kind and gentle parents, but I parted from them when I was just seven years old. At that time, I left for Tsurphu Monastery, the traditional seat of the Karmapa in central Tibet, where I would receive all the training I needed as the Karmapa. It takes two or three days to travel from our valley to the capital city of Lhasa, so my parents only used to come to see me once or twice a year. Leaving your parents at such a young age can be very disorienting. I felt really strange at times. But slowly I recognized that perhaps my biological parents were not the only parents I had. Many others cared for and helped me. I could have *benefiting parents* as well as *biological parents*. They could be as far away as America or Europe and still offer me lots of love and support and even material gifts. I came to feel the closeness of a family relationship to them as well. I had this direct experience, and it showed me that it really is possible to see anyone as our parent.

Once we decide we want to do so, we find many ways to create a vast sense of human community that can transcend all barriers. From our family to our friends on up, communities of various sizes offer intermediate steps as we gradually enlarge our circle of compassion and empathy, until we finally reach a global level. We can start to feel that the world is a big family—a big community—and the planet is our big home. We can see each other as family members.

If we could recognize and feel that all beings are our fathers, mothers, brothers, sisters, friends, and neighbors, then without ever needing to go online, we would already have the basis for making community anywhere, with anyone. The boundaries between communities can disappear when we strengthen our more basic connectedness. We ourselves must dissolve these boundaries. To live interdependence is to experience our human community as boundless.

ELEVEN

Lenses for Global Society

T HE WHOLE WORLD seems to have fallen under the sway of globalization. Before, from one valley to the next, there could be notable differences in what people ate or wore and in what people raised their children to value. Ways of living differed much more from place to place. But now the forces of globalization and consumerism are working together to bring everyone in a single direction. What if it turns out not to be the right direction?

The aim of this book is to calm our minds and think more clearly and carefully about the direction we are going. We cannot simply continue indefinitely in the direction we are currently heading. We have abundant evidence that this is not sustainable, but we are recognizing this fact at a fortunate moment. An awareness of the need for change is increasingly widespread. Our exploitation of the planet's natural resources has not yet brought us to a point of no return. The time to change course is now.

The intensity of exchange of information and ideas that is made possible by technology intensifies our connectedness, but it by no means guarantees that we will choose the best course of action for living together as a global community. Our current global pursuit of consumer goods and consumerist values is only one option. To explore other, more realistic and sustainable models for our global society, we can start by looking at how we are conceiving our global relationships.

Many conversations about society today use terms like *global citizen*, *global family*, and *global village* to emphasize how we are united in a universal human community. These ways of conceiving of our relationship each have a somewhat different emotional content. We feel and behave differently toward someone we consider to be a friend compared to a fellow citizen or family member. Since the model we apply affects how we feel about them and therefore how we interact with them, it also affects the type of global society we are creating.

Since we are connected in diverse ways, it makes sense that we have diverse ways to understand and experience that connectedness. It is a bit like having different lenses that let us see different colors and facets of reality. In this chapter, we will try on the lenses of global citizens, global family, and global friends to explore what each one can bring into focus. As we proceed, we will need to ensure that whatever model we follow is fully inclusive and does not privilege any particular segment of that global society. To that end, we will also identify the considerable work that would be needed to apply any given model universally and equitably.

LENS 1: GLOBAL CITIZENSHIP

The term *global citizenship* helps bring some valuable aspects of reality into view. First, it emphasizes the fact that we all share rights and responsibilities as inhabitants of the same planet. Too often we fail to look past the national borders that divide one country's citizens from another's. Interdependence does not stop at national borderlines.

Within our planet's ecosystem, our interdependence crosses boundaries constantly—in fact, it absolutely ignores them. We may seek to export the causes of environmental disaster outside our national territory when we ship our waste to other countries or when we invest in harmful manufacturing processes in other countries that are banned in our own. When we think of the whole planet as our territory, we see that there is nowhere to safely allow such destruction. We are not damaging anyone's home but our own. We can extend such an analysis to our planet's social "ecosystem" as well.

Every human being has an equal right to live on this planet and thus can be considered a global citizen. The idea of global citizenship helps us recognize that we are dwelling together in a single planetary home. It also alerts us to the fact that all human beings have equal rights to the planet's resources, and that we must therefore find ways to share the planet. But acknowledging that right does not automatically mean we uphold it; sharing is not always easy. We need to feel a connection and a commitment to one another in order to be willing to share the world's resources. This is especially true when sharing requires changing our behavior or making do with less.

A question I have is whether thinking of ourselves as global citizens can generate the authentic caring about others needed to bring about actual sharing of resources and opportunities. To me, at least, the term *global citizenship* evokes a legalistic image. It makes me think of rights, laws, and obligations. I imagine a global capital with a global bureaucracy issuing global passports. My point is not to weigh the feasibility of a single global governing body. My concern here is the mental and emotional impact of applying the model of citizenship to our global relationships. What kinds of feelings does it evoke or obstruct?

When we draw on our experience of being a citizen of a particular country to see how we relate to one another when we are relating as fellow citizens, we will see that this varies a great deal. For many refugees, people who are stateless or who otherwise hold no passport, the idea of citizenship may not evoke any sense of equality and inclusion. Certainly it will not evoke the same experiences and feelings it evokes for citizens of powerful countries. This means that the term *global citizen* is not appealing to a basis of experience we all share, and this could limit its usefulness in pointing out a relationship we all share.

Broadly speaking, citizens within a single country do not necessarily support or actively work to benefit each other simply because they are fellow citizens. They may well feel like strangers to each other. Citizens are not often connected by bonds of warmth and closeness. People who are citizens might act with kindness to one another but most likely not simply because they are fellow citizens. Human beings do take care of one another as human beings. But as citizens, they generally look to the government to take care of their needs, through its embassies and other institutional structures. Citizens receive care as a right and share resources as an obligation. This responsibility to share is typically imposed by law or external authority. In this sense, thinking of our global relationships as citizens might end up reinforcing our sense of being separate individuals regulated by the same laws rather than encouraging us to feel and embrace our interdependence.

Citizens do pull together and recognize their common bonds when they perceive a common enemy. As global citizens, we do face common threats in the form of humanitarian and environmental crises. But these threats are not coming from outside humanity. We ourselves are creating them.

This complicates the process of creating a fellow feeling among global citizens, because identifying ourselves as citizens often comes from a feeling of *us* in contrast to some *them*. As we see during national elections, our habitual manner of expressing patriotism can awaken xenophobia, which is certainly not a sentiment consistent with the reality of interdependence!

For these reasons, the idea of citizenship, while useful for underscoring our equal condition as residents of this planet, might not readily scale up to a global level or create the feelings of closeness or the culture of inclusivity that interdependence suggests.

A final—and key—question is whether seeing our global community through the lens of citizenship will inspire us to live our interdependence. Is modeling our connection to others on citizenship the best foundation for cultivating an open heart and mind, strengthening our empathy and compassion, and sustaining our motivation to make positive changes in our global human community? This is worth asking ourselves.

LENS 2: GLOBAL FAMILY

I recognize that not everyone has had the same warm family environment that I had the great good fortune to have enjoyed in my childhood. However, as we discussed above, it is within the family that we gain our most immediate experiences of being connected to others. When we see another person as family, we feel closely connected. This gives us the opportunity to feel that vital truth of interdependence—that others are part of who we are and that we are part of others. Until this awareness permeates our hearts, we will not have the inner foundation we need to be able to truly live our interdependence. This makes thinking of ourselves as a global family especially promising.

The sense of family can be so powerful that it extends to people we have never met without this diminishing our concern for their welfare whatsoever. We could have cousins or other distant relatives whose names we do not even know but whom we still greet warmly at family gatherings. As I noted above, this expandable sense of connectedness is not so easy to generate using the model of global citizenship. This is why thinking of one another as family holds such promise for enhancing our emotional awareness of our interdependence.

Within a family, it is easy to see how profoundly we affect one another, for good or bad. One person's troubles are naturally felt by all, just as one person's happiness and success brings a shared sense of joy. In our families, we experience the profound truth that joy and happiness increase most when they are shared, while sorrows too are lightened by being shared.

Within a family, caretaking for one another happens spontaneously and willingly rather than as a matter of duty imposed by law or external authority. Although sadly it does happen on occasion, it is very much the exception that the law needs to intervene to get parents to care for their children. I think the reason we find it so hard to countenance the instances when this does happen is because love and concern for children usually do arise naturally.

We look to those we consider family to feel cherished and loved. We do not ask whether we are biologically related to those who cared for us. If we recall the person who picked us up when we cried, carried us when we were tired, bathed us and combed our hair, dressed us and tied our shoes when we were small, that person feels like family whether or not we are blood relations. It is a warmth of feeling that binds us together as family. When we feel connected as family, caring and being cared for arise easily.

When we view our global interdependence through the lens of family, it encourages us to reflect on the many ways that we are cared for by others, especially in our most vulnerable moments. We only survived the earliest stages of life because we had someone who cared for us responsibly and generously in countless ways.

Our parents and other caretakers do not rest once they have supplied the material resources needed for our survival. Not only do they provide for our physical needs, equally or more importantly, such caregivers encourage and protect our inner resources. Although I have undergone a good deal of formal training to prepare me for my role as the Karmapa, my first formative moral and spiritual education took place before I was recognized as the Karmapa, within my family. When we were very small, my mother and father took pains to teach us to feel how precious life was and to respect and cherish all forms of life, whether big or small. I have six sisters, all of them older than me, and I remember one day I went to a river with the youngest of my sisters. We were careless and inadvertently killed a ladybug. When we saw what we had done, we were able to recognize the fatal suffering we had caused by this small act, one that otherwise people might dismiss without a second thought.

Because of how we were raised by our parents, we felt keenly the importance of this lost life and our role in taking it, and wanted very much to be able to do something for this small being. We decided we must at least give the ladybug a proper funeral, so we stayed there through our lunchtime, making it a series of small burial mounds called *stupas*. This is a customary Tibetan way to honor and care for the deceased. As I look back on such experiences, it is clear to me that my mother and father were nurturing my inner qualities. In fact, they were my first spiritual guides.

We might each have comparable memories from our childhood, when our parents' encouragement enabled us to connect with our nobler qualities—our natural empathy or sense of responsibility for others. We were unlikely aware that our parents were acting as teachers in the cultivation of inner resources. With reflection, however, we can surely identify numerous family experiences that contributed in one way or another to our moral and spiritual growth.

Even if we come up with examples in which we feel that our family life negatively impacted the growth of our inner qualities, this only serves to underscore the importance of the collective impact we have on one another. Seeing ourselves as a family shows us how much is at stake in caring for all members of our society. We can feel how crucial it is for global society to provide conditions for all its members to cultivate their positive personal qualities. If we could learn to extend it to the entire human community, the sense of connectedness that arises in families could become an excellent basis for those qualities to grow within each of us.

Like family, friendships can evoke the sense of closeness that we need to develop toward the rest of the human community. In some cases we can actually be too close to family members to see the depth and intensity of those connections or to see how much we receive from them. Especially in the case of parents or those adults who cared for us since we were small, we often take their care for granted.

Say our older relatives give us a gift of clothing. They hope that we will wear it and sincerely think it will look good on us. But their gift does not match our ideas of fashion, and so we choose not to wear it. In Tibetan culture, in such situations our older relatives might say to us, "When I am dead, you can wear whatever you want!" They may live on a fixed income and may have had to splurge a bit to purchase the gift for us. But we feel no need to reciprocate with efforts of our own, precisely because we do not notice the effort and affection behind their gesture. We may end up hurting them by taking their gestures of love for granted.

By contrast, in friendships we recognize more readily the value of investing time and effort and can appreciate more deeply what we are offered. The emotional bond can be more apparent to us. While some friendships may arise merely from prolonged contact, generally friendships have a greater element of intentional choice and conscious commitment than family relationships.

The profound impact that friends can have on one another is underscored in the use of the language of friendship to describe the role of spiritual guides in Buddhism. The relationship between a guru and disciple is not likened to an ordinary teacher-and-student relationship but is understood primarily as a friendship. In English, you say *spiritual teacher*, but within Buddhism the term used literally means "virtuous friend" or "friend in virtue."

The emotional or mental connection between disciple and spiritual guide, or virtuous friend, is the most important element in the relationship. Less important is how often one meets in person or how many hours of direct instruction one receives. The physical care received, too, plays a far smaller role in this relationship than it does in the family. Even the exact words exchanged are not crucial. The disciple-guide relationship develops on a much deeper level than that.

It is more like a friendship than a teacher-student relationship also in the sense that the relationship is not limited to certain circumstances, such as the classroom or the time during which the person is enrolled in courses with them. Thinking of the spiritual relationship as a form of friendship helps us see that, once established, friendships continue to shape us throughout our lives even if the conditions of our lives change and we are no longer able to interact directly. This offers us valuable perspectives as we seek to maintain global relationships. Although direct contact has a power of its own, as we have seen, nevertheless we do not need to interact physically or verbally in order to be having a formative effect on one another. The encouragement we received in a critical moment from a childhood friend may still be a source of support to us even if our life has changed considerably.

Similarly, we are particularly inclined to see our friends' positive sides. Our friends will not be perfect, but we naturally view them favorably and focus more on their positive qualities—the ones we like and respect. Between spiritual teacher and disciple in Buddhism, as between regular friends, the disciple recognizes the positive qualities of the teacher on an emotional level and develops an appreciation and a feeling for them, just as the teacher is committed to the growth of the disciple's positive qualities as well.

Like a bee that goes straight to the sweet nectar of a flower and does not trouble itself with whatever dust or dirt might surround it, with friends we learn to enjoy what we like and not look for faults. It does not mean there is no awareness of shortcomings; rather we are willing to be the person's ally in fighting their faults. We do not reject them simply because we notice a blemish. We put their faults in context because we keep most prominently in mind all that we have found to admire and enjoy in them.

We could choose to offer this same generosity of judgment to those we do not consider friends, by looking beyond their external behavior and seeking out the underlying positive qualities that we know lie within them. We can always recall that any negative conduct or attitudes we observe will have their own causes and conditions and do not reflect that totality of the person, as discussed earlier. When we want to, we can always find another vantage point from which to find something with which to connect in others. It is a matter of conscious effort and gradual training.

We could train ourselves to apply the lens of friendship in other types of relationships as well. How would this work? Look for what you want to engage with in the other. Do not seek out what you do not want.

WIDENING THE LENS

Each of the three models offers us a somewhat different lens for understanding, feeling, and developing our relationships with others in the human community. Whichever model we are using, we need to sustain the feeling of connectedness and responsibility that arises in our friendships or family, as we extend that same lens further to include an increasingly wider community. We ourselves need to be able to expand outward with our heart and mind.

In Tibetan we have a saying: "One enemy is too many. One hundred friends are too few." We try to live by this saying and engage in particular practices that help us do so. Other religious traditions will have their own practices that take different forms but share similar aims. Many of these Buddhist practices could be equally used by people with no commitment to a Buddhist path, because they have little to do with doctrinal beliefs but rather involve working on our basic human attitudes and relationships. They allow us to see and feel more openness and more warmth toward others.

How do we generate such attitudes and feelings for another human being? There are two ways for this feeling of cherishing others and holding them dear to grow within us. One arises spontaneously, without any special effort. The other arises through training—through intentionally cultivating that feeling. The Buddhist practices that seek to give rise to such feelings take as their starting point the existing natural feelings of affection we already feel toward some people and consciously build on them.

The goal is to be able to experience the same tenderness and affection toward all sentient beings equally. We want our attitude toward them to be loving at the same time as they become so dear to our heart that we feel that if anything pained them, it would be unbearable for us. This is possible when we have cultivated a sense of authentic closeness to them. With it, we are drawn to that person and sincerely and intensely care for them. Without it, we would not cherish them so deeply.

Everyone already has a basis for this training in enhancing our innate positive emotions. It is just a matter of building upon that base—stabilizing the existing affection and active concern we feel for our close friends and family and learning how to consciously extend these toward others. In the last chapter, I mentioned one method used in this context, that of seeing all beings as our mothers and gradually learning to direct the same love toward any sentient being that we feel naturally toward our mother or other dearly loved one.

A subsequent step toward connecting with the entire human community in this way is to break down barriers that mark us off, so that we can extend our sense of closeness to all others equally. The first barrier to tackle is the strong sense of separation between self and other, which we can dismantle by reflecting deeply on the many ways others are integral to who we are, as outlined in chapter 1.

A further barrier is the strong tendency to discriminate based on our own likes and dislikes. One Buddhist technique for overcoming such discrimination can be found as part of a practice called the four immeasurables: immeasurable love, immeasurable compassion, immeasurable joy, and immeasurable equanimity. These qualities are called immeasurable because they can be extended infinitely, beyond all measure. We list them in this order, but what we cultivate first is equanimity, which can be defined as an emotional awareness of our radical equality. This method draws attention to the way that we normally divide the entire human population based on our own feelings toward them. We invite some people into our circle of friends, exclude those we dislike, and remain indifferent to everyone else. As we cultivate equanimity, we are developing our ability to feel the same sense of closeness and affection toward people we find annoying and people we do not know as we do toward our loved ones.

This practice encourages us to recognize that these divisions are ultimately arbitrary and untenable. All beings wish to be happy and do not wish to suffer. When it comes to the right to happiness and freedom from suffering that we all share equally, the sense of *us* and *them* has no relevance whatsoever. We can find endless differences in our group identities, starting with nationality, race, gender, and religion, but in this more basic sense—the root—we could not be more equal.

This is not to deny that some communities or peoples have been targeted for persecution because they have been labeled as different or deficient. Minority communities in every society are subjected to prejudice and abuse at the hands of other communities. Their yearning to be free of such mistreatment could be more acute and enduring than your longing to be free of whatever forms of suffering you are experiencing at the moment. We are all equal, but if anyone is to warrant greater attention, it is those who have an even more urgent longing to be free of suffering and an even greater wish for happiness than you do, because they are more deprived of happiness than you are. We share the world with many people who face more severe personal obstacles than we do or who are oppressed by pervasive social discrimination that robs them of the conditions they need to escape their suffering and find happiness. By actively cultivating positive feelings toward all others universally, we can find the resolve to seek out ways to end such suffering.

WORKING WITH AVERSION

As we move toward implementing a vision of a global society, we will certainly encounter inner obstacles as well as outer. As we look within, we discover forces that make it difficult for us personally to view everyone equally. Aversion and attachment are two destructive inner conditions that lead us to divide up humanity, pushing some people away and drawing others near. If we are to connect with all our fellow global citizens, family members, or friends in a way that reflects our equality, we will need to combat the twin obstacles of attachment and aversion.

We may feel animosity toward some people due to their behavior or attitudes. If someone harms us, we can fault their particular action or motivation, but if we label the entire person as bad, then we are also maligning and denying whatever positive qualities they have, including all their latent goodness. This is disrespectful toward the person, but it is also disrespectful toward actual reality. We are calling faulty what is not faulty. We need to be clear that we are disagreeing with a specific behavior or attitude, and not dismissing the person as a whole. There is far more to them than what we perceive them to be in any given situation.

In any case, someone who is your enemy in one moment and in one situation is not your eternal enemy. As causes and conditions shift, their actions will also change. At any moment, they can and will behave differently. The action is transitory. The person lives on.

Sometimes the fact that someone is acting as your enemy could be a sign he or she needs more care. Of course, there are many cases where it is just the hostility you feel toward them that makes someone appear to you as your enemy. But it could also well be that they act hostilely toward you because they are suffering and need more happiness. Their behavior may be driven by insecurity, fear, or misguided strategies to gain happiness. Their very appearance to you as difficult could be directly indicating that they need more comfort, care, or support.

Homeless people or others who have fallen on difficult times can be seen at intersections of big cities all around the world. Some of them can be quite aggressive, verbally or even physically. They may tap on your window or splash water on your windshield to induce you to offer them some cash. Some may seem dissatisfied no matter how much you give. You may feel they are acting as if you had their money inside your car and were about to drive off with it.

We might feel annoyed by their persistence, but this is actually a sign of the intensity of their desperation, their distress, and their hunger for happiness. This is not a matter of imagining or pretending that they suffer more in order to lessen our resentment. In many cases, they actually *are* suffering more.

Along with considering what people need, we also have to look at the intensity of their craving to have that need met. We have different forms of suffering, but even among those who share the same painful conditions, different people experience different degrees of desperation to escape their situation. There will be people with greater needs than us. But there will also be people with the same or fewer actual needs who feel more keenly than we do their lack of happiness and suffer more as a result. Their yearning for happiness is greater than ours.

This is an important aspect of learning to live in an interdependent world as equals who are not all the same. While we are equal in terms of our basic human needs, our perceptions of our own situation can differ. Different people experience the same outer conditions differently. It is the interplay of inner conditions and outer conditions that shapes any given situation. How we interpret our experiences shapes those very experiences, and it shapes how we act based upon them. This is another reason paying attention to inner conditions is so powerful in initiating change in the world.

Once we have consciously embraced the goal of protecting our ability to respect and feel affection for each person, we can adopt whichever technique we find most effective. Whenever we notice aversion arising in us, we can intentionally drop our excessive fixation on the behavior or attitudes that we regard as harmful and instead connect to whatever positive we trust that the person has within them. When we stay open to the whole person, we can always find something positive to connect to. At the very least, we can connect to them with confidence in their inner potential.

WORKING WITH ATTACHMENT

The flip side of aversion is attachment, which leads us to cling to certain people and want to keep them close, to the exclusion of others. Buddhist texts use the analogy of a silkworm that hangs onto its silk and thereby traps itself in its own web. We become stuck in our own attachment. With attachment, driven by personal desire and self-interest, we trap ourselves. No one else does it to us. Starting where we are now, it is not practical to say we must do away with all attachment entirely. But it is important to recognize how harmful it is and diminish it wherever possible.

When we have strong attachment, we are not fully open to the person. Often we are actually not all that interested in listening to the details of what the other person feels or thinks. What interests us is for them to listen to us. We only really want to hear what we'd like them to tell us, not what they want to say. This underlying orientation makes us act like the more important person in that relationship. We feel as if those we are attached to owe it to us to fulfill our wishes. When we have this sort of attachment inside us, it serves as a condition for anger to easily arise. We can see this in families, where if we do not get what we want from others, we become quite angry or disappointed in them.

Attachment is about me. It is about what I can get from the other person or other things. Love is about the other person. Whereas attachment is self-centered, love is other-oriented. Attachment is about the fulfillment of my self-interests. Love cares about the other's needs. Both for the sake of our own peace and satisfaction in life and for the sake of our global society, we need to reduce the scope we give to attachment. Our first step is to become aware of its presence in our attitudes and interactions, and then consciously and actively begin to adopt the opposing attitude of love.

UNCONDITIONAL LOVE

However we conceptualize our global relations, whether as fellow citizens, family members, or friends, it will take a great deal of patient effort to extend it to every single being. Mental agility will be invaluable as we shift to whatever inner vantage points allow us to sustain our altruism in any given situation. But that is the goal: to expand our benevolent orientation until it is as inclusive as reality itself and stabilize it until we can maintain it in any and all circumstances.

In Tibetan Buddhism, we train to be able to make this commitment to care for others the very center of our lives. We call those who are sincerely engaging in such training in altruism *bodhisattvas*. Bodhisattvas' training in altruism is based on giving 100 percent of themselves. They do not give 99 percent of themselves freely and then look to be compensated for giving the remaining 1 percent.

One of the most revered figures in Tibetan Buddhism is Milarepa, an eleventh-century yogi who undertook this bodhisattva training in earnest. He lived alone in caves, in remote and desolated mountains where the temperature often dropped below zero. Milarepa survived by eating nettles and whatever else he found to hand in his barren surroundings. In his own day and time, his form of spiritual practice was considered extreme, and some people thought he was crazy. His own sister told him, "I have seen a lot of other spiritual practitioners, but none of them live anything like you. I do not know whether you have it wrong or they have it wrong, but I do know you are going to die if you keep up like this." But Milarepa kept going, following the path he had committed to in order to fulfill his bodhisattva training.

What Milarepa did, every moment of every day, was work on his mind. Nothing else. He engaged in this practice for the benefit of sentient beings, offering every thought to others and every breath to others. He did not live like this for himself. This simple yogi began every action with the wish to be of benefit to others, then he engaged in the action with others in mind, and in the end he dedicated the fruits of whatever he had done to the welfare of all. Nobody knew that he was doing this for them. He just pursued his practices by himself in all the isolated places he stayed—meditating and praying with great enthusiasm, dedicating the results of his practice to others. Despite the extreme conditions, he often sang songs that arose spontaneously from his heart to express the profound joy he felt at being able to live that way.

Milarepa's example shows what is possible when we live with our intentions directed entirely toward others, even if our work is entirely internal and done alone. He held no hope for recognition or for any external reward. The inner rewards were so rich that he was sustained by them even amid great hardship and privation. A millennium later, the story of his life is still often retold, and his example continues to inspire and teach us.

Other people might not know you are doing anything for them, but this does not prevent you from extending your love to them. Of course, the love we can offer now is mixed with self-interest, but we can slowly improve the quality of that love, reducing the elements of attachment and self-importance that creep in. Reciprocity is not required. If we wait for others to love us first, that might never happen. Just as when we act from generosity, we can give our love with no expectation of reward. The joy of giving is reward enough. The love we feel itself warms us. Like those heat packets people carry in their pockets in cold climates to warm their hands, we can reach inside and find something within to warm ourselves. We can urge ourselves on, and give ourselves our own approval and encouragement. Milarepa gave everything he had to others, even though there was no one there to recognize that fact and praise him for it. He did so because he understood that this is what matters—holding nothing back in extending oneself to others.

The key thing is to enjoy the goodness of what you are doing and feeling. Enjoy the sensation of filling your own heart with love and then offering it to others. You begin by first savoring the warmheartedness that you give rise to, and only then expressing and extending it toward others. If it is not warming for you, how can you know it will be warming for others?

If you are not really enjoying your own feeling of warm-heartedness and love, you are left feeling empty if others do not appreciate it or reciprocate when you offer it to them. But love does not work like a business deal. Once you learn to delight in the love you hold within yourself, you can always have a full heart. You can fill yourself with love.

Even if Milarepa is an extreme case and not a lifestyle we can realistically adopt, the example of his life does show us the possibility of embracing our connectedness to all others, equally and without exception.

But this is not the only reason I mention him. The life of Milarepa also shows that we have options that may not have occurred to us before. The example of Milarepa remains with us today not as a sign that we should follow the path that he chose, but rather as a sign that the best path for us could be a path no one else has chosen.

The models of global relationship we have reviewed also let us see that we have options. There is more than one route forward. In the end, however we choose to move toward it, the goal is to live with interdependence in a way that can sustain us all as we each cultivate our inner resources and make our diverse contributions to the world we share equally.

What sort of life gives more satisfaction and is more meaningful? That is the question we need to ask ourselves as we move ahead. Once we have the goal clear, wherever we are, we can always change course so that we keep moving toward it.

TWELVE

Linking Aspirations

Happiness is not just a feeling of excitement or passing joy. Although often taken to be happiness, such fleeting pleasures depend upon external conditions and are not long-lasting or stable. Conditions inevitably change over time. This is the reality of impermanence. The happiness we ultimately seek must last beyond transitory feelings and circumstances.

My own aspiration is for all beings to be able to find such authentic happiness, a lasting happiness that cannot be dislodged by the whims of shifting conditions. True happiness is not superficial or fleeting. It is complete freedom from any reason to suffer. By addressing the very causes of suffering and bringing together the very causes of happiness, it becomes possible to reach such a state. To go beyond ordinary happiness and suffering, beyond the limitations of our immediate experience, even beyond birth and death, the causes of happiness must be joined with wisdom.

As I have been emphasizing, the resources needed to fulfill our individual and collective aspirations are inner resources, and these are endlessly renewable. One of the most precious of these inner resources is our capacity for discernment, and we need to use this ability to distinguish between what is superficial and what is real, what leads to true happiness and what does not.

The world we have built rests on an unrealistic expectation that when our material development reaches its peak, we will all be happy. The world has been applying its best brains and best efforts to advancing material development, and this has not yielded the lasting happiness we all seek. Yet our globalized society keeps rushing together toward that idyllic destination we seem to believe awaits us just a little further ahead. This illusory dream leads us to spend our days chasing outer goods. It reinforces our belief that our happiness relies on external conditions. At the same time, it obscures and devalues the powerful inner resources we have that could actually allow us to realize our aspirations. The shortcoming is not in our efforts but in the limitations of the material we are working with. External goods are simply not what real happiness is made from. No physical techniques in the world, no matter how clever or effective, can generate an inner sense of well-being.

Everything we have seen about interdependence tells us that this expectation—that we can arrange for happiness by arranging things around us in just the right way—is not only unrealistic but also has grave, ongoing consequences for our global society. Our planet cannot sustain the relentless and escalating demands on its natural resources. Only deepening our definition of happiness and fundamentally reorienting our relationship to nature and to other living beings can establish harmony.

Competing for limited resources as a means to find happiness also leads us to imagine that happiness too is a limited resource—that our happiness comes at the cost of others' happiness and freedom, and that others' true happiness and freedom will detract from our own. Life becomes a battle of self against others, us against them.

Focusing so much on external circumstances accentuates our differences and obscures our fundamental and profound equality. As we constantly compete and compare, we begin to see difference as deficiency. We come to feel that we are essentially different from others, which harms our ability to connect. It reinforces the mistaken view that we are ultimately separate and independent individuals. As our empathy starts to shut down, the walls close in around us. We become blind to the beauty and strength of diversity. We do not see our own beauty reflected in others; in fact, we hardly see others at all.

The beauty is there, and others are certainly there, no matter how nearsighted we have made ourselves. The task I have been proposing is a matter of learning to look in new ways, so that we can truly see and feel the presence of others with us in the world and ground our actions in our connectedness to them. An important aspiration of this book is to contribute to this shift in perspective, the fundamental shift that comes about when we live our lives with an emotional awareness of our interdependence.

PLANTING ASPIRATIONS

From the moment we are born, we are endowed with an innate capacity to empathize, to care compassionately for others. This means we have a natural basis for living as emotionally interdependent individuals. As we have seen, there are many ways we can work with this innate capacity in order to make it manifest. Generating and acting on virtuous intentions is one part of the process of nurturing that potential, but beyond specific intentions, we need to strengthen and stabilize the noble aspirations that will sustain us over the long term. We need to nourish them continually.

Aspirations orient us in life. We can hold them in our hearts even when there is no opportunity to act on them in that particular moment. They can guide our intentions and our actions but are larger than either of the two. An intention determines the particular end to which an action is directed. When you act intentionally, your mind and deeds are aimed in a single direction. Aspirations are more enduring than intentions, providing a larger sense of purpose that suggests the course that our particular intentions and actions should take. When you have major decisions to make, you can reflect on your aspirations in life to determine which specific intentions you would need to generate and act on in order to fulfill those aspirations.

In Tibetan the verb that we use for cultivating aspirations is *planting*. This reminds us that our work is just beginning when a seed is sown. When it is a tender sprout, we recognize how fragile it is and so we protect it. As the shoot grows, we cannot afford to neglect it, but must keep caring for it as it gradually becomes a full-grown tree yielding blossoms and fruits. Our aspirations are the same. Only if we consciously nurture them will they become firmly rooted in our hearts and bear fruit in our lives.

We could also treat our aspirations as beloved children. When we give birth to something of great value and beauty, we should care for it as a loving mother would. As a mother, we wish to hold our precious children close and nourish them with our whole being. In the same way, we do not want to pass our tender young aspirations off to someone else; we want to keep them close and nurture them ourselves. Nor do we want to just apply the occasional forceful push but then neglect our aspirations the rest of the time. We want to keep them moving along steadily, well beyond momentary bursts of enthusiasm.

Aspirations grow gradually, and so tending them requires patience and perseverance. First, we arouse noble and positive aspirations that we did not previously have. Next, we stabilize them and extend their scope. As we then intensify their strength, our aspirations become a force that shapes the specific intentions that propel us into action.

Deepening our awareness of interdependence not only changes our point of view. It stirs new feelings and motivates us to new courses of intentional action. Our aspirations themselves change and become more expansive. What we aspire to is no longer limited to outer achievements but also extends to inner achievements. As our awareness opens to include the vast interconnectedness within which our lives unfold, our aspirations can and should open as well.

NOT LOSING HEART

Everyone has the idea to do something virtuous at different moments. We have thoughts of spending time with an elderly neighbor, making space in our home for a refugee who lost her parents when their boat overturned, or working to protect freshwater sources. Although such thoughts arise of benefiting someone else and making a positive contribution to the world, we also meet with obstacles in enacting our virtuous plans. If we do not have enough courage, we start to lose heart. We think, "This won't work. I can't do this."

In a sense, this is a bit selfish. I have observed this in my own experience. If I try to do something to help others and things do not seem to be working out, the thought can arise, "I can't make this happen." This is the moment when we are at risk for withdrawing our efforts. In one way, it is understandable that we might experience this. If we cannot accomplish something, we do have to know when to let go. However, when we give up on our plans to benefit others, more often than not it is because of egocentrism. It happens when we are looking at things purely from our own perspective.

When we look at the situation from the perspective of others, we can see how urgently our help is needed. Our thoughts of acting to benefit arose precisely because we saw that they were suffering and something needed to be done. Given what it means to the elderly neighbor, the refugee girl, and to all those who need clean drinking water, how can we give up? Seen from this angle, it simply does not appear as an option to throw up our hands and abandon them to their loneliness and thirst.

Switching points of view like this—to see things from the perspective of those who need us to act—can boost our courage immensely. The principle of interdependence shows us that we can look at any situation from multiple angles, and that many vantage points can be valid and mutually enriching. Learning to live interdependence as a value involves becoming more adept at adopting new points of view. Feeling connected to those who hold those points of view allows us to shift from one position to another naturally. Wisdom helps us know when it is time to shift to another vantage point.

Do not let yourself get stuck. When your motivation wanes, apply your wisdom and mental flexibility and try seeing it from the other side. Your side only has one person waiting for his or her aims to be accomplished, but the other side has many people all longing to fulfill their aims of finding happiness and escaping suffering. Sometimes looking at the needs of others gives you the added courage you need to keep going toward your noble aims. Sometimes you just find the courage within yourself. You can use either approach, and you can also alternate between them. If you are looking at it from the perspective of others but your courage still seems lacking, then look at it from the perspective of your own personal aspirations. If your own aspirations do not lend the needed force to your courage, try focusing on what others aspire to. This is how to apply wisdom to increase your mental agility and actively nurture your own tender aspirations.

ASPIRING FOR SELF AND OTHER

People sometimes ask me how to balance their own personal goals for themselves with their larger goals for the world. If you are caught up in habits of selfishness, your personal goals might conflict with your larger goals for the world. If your personal goals are healthy—which means consistent with interdependence—then they will naturally have a positive effect on the world.

Your flourishing will surely contribute to the larger goal of helping others flourish. Because we all exist interdependently, we ourselves are a part of others and others are a part of us. Don't think that there is a vast gap between yourself and others, or between your personal goals and the larger aims of benefiting the world. These are inseparable.

If you fully understand that these various aims are inseparable from one another, you can avoid a great deal of confusion in life. You will not find yourself in endless quandaries having to choose between your personal aims and the aspirations you have for the world.

Living a happy, wholesome life and making your own life meaningful will automatically have a positive impact on others. For one, your flourishing will contribute to the happiness of all those who care for you. It will also increase the collective happiness of all the communities you are part of. Ultimately, it will benefit the entire human community.

THE MUSIC OF CHANGE

Thanks to impermanence, we never need to feel stuck. The fact that things are changing all the time means that we live in a constant state of possibility. Just because we were cranky and unhappy in the morning does not mean we will be cranky in the afternoon. We might just as easily be cheerful and content in the evening. Change brings opportunity. Just because someone did something bad in the past, there is no reason to say they are a bad person now. Every moment is a fresh opportunity. Every instant is a new life. You get a chance to begin anew every single moment. You can discover new meanings, give birth to new aspirations, or act at last to fulfill long-held dreams.

This is possible when we live with a vivid awareness of the impermanence of our lives. A few years ago, a group of schoolchildren were killed in a massacre in Norway. Speaking to a journalist a year or so later, one of the survivors, a fifteen-year-old girl, said that every day since then, her first thought when she wakes up has been that that could be the last day of her life. She said that many people might think that this is a dark and depressing way to think, but to her there is nothing gloomy about it.

People do often focus on the negative. Looking at impermanence, they see that nothing lasts and that we are all going to die. That thought strikes them as rather bleak, and so they shy away from acknowledging the transitory nature of things. However, this is not a question of positive or negative; it is reality, and we always ignore reality at our own risk. Acknowledging the fact of constant change could just as easily be a positive and beneficial way to think.

Take the example of a flute. If it made only one sound continuously, that single unwavering sound would not be especially pleasing. It would certainly not be music. The possibility of music—its beauty—is rooted directly in the reality of impermanence. The sound changes from one note to another and in this lies the essence of music. Without this transitory nature of all phenomena, we would be stuck on one note, eternally!

As a result, rather than discouraging or overwhelming us, an awareness of impermanence should actually make our aspirations grow. Knowing that things will not always be as they are now can inspire us to dream of how else things could be. It gives us fertile ground to plant new aspirations. Impermanence can work against stagnation. By the afternoon, the aspirations we planted in the morning could have put down deep roots. Each following day, we could revisit and strengthen that aspiration. The very first moment the conditions arise to implement them, our aspirations will have carried us right into the thick of the most productive action.

Just because we have not yet fulfilled our dreams is no reason to think that we will not do so in the future. New possibilities are unfolding continuously. A heightened awareness of impermanence keeps us alert to the many possible futures that are opening before us. Our aspirations can guide us in determining which opportunity to take in order to create the future we want.

Every single moment we are simultaneously starting a new future but also bringing the past to an irrevocable end. Normally we think of death as the major end that comes when we draw our last breath, but that is only the most obvious form of death. The reality is that we experience death in its more subtle forms every day, all day. Things are ending all the time. We wake up in the morning and the life we led the previous day is gone; there is absolutely no way to get it back. But in that very moment, we are also born into a whole new life that begins right then. With that new life, we can always give rise to new aspirations, and renew those we wish to keep present.

A PLACE FOR THE IMPOSSIBLE

Aspirations are a powerful force leading us to grow beyond our current capacities. The ability to determine to surpass what is now a limitation is another of our limitless inner resources. The reality of interdependence means that the range of what is possible is vaster than we ordinarily recognize. As we have seen, even small changes in one condition affect the final outcome. We constantly set off ever-expanding ripples of change, as conditions adjust to accommodate each shift. This dynamic and fluid interplay of causes and effects brings endless waves of entirely fresh possibilities.

What's more, our aspirations need not be contained even by what is humanly possible. As enduring guides for our intentions and actions, aspirations can be worth nurturing even if we can never accomplish them. I described bodhisattvas—people who seek to make their altruistic aspirations the very essence of their lives. Such noble beings nurture two types of aspirations—those that can be fulfilled and those that cannot be fulfilled.

The first are our usual, straightforward hopes and wishes, such as the aspiration to do well on an exam or for someone to recover their health. These are all within the realm of the possible.

The second type of aspirations comprises those that we will never be able to accomplish. These include such aspirations as to be able to end world hunger even if we have to do it all by ourselves, or for everyone suffering from depression to be instantly filled with joy and hope. With such aspirations, we give our imaginations the freedom to move beyond the boundaries of what we know to be possible. Even though such aspirations are not feasible and cannot possibly be fulfilled, nonetheless we should definitely continue making such aspirations.

Even though we know they will never result in the external conditions we imagine, such aspirations create important inner conditions. They open and fortify our heart. They strengthen our courage and determination. It is one thing to give rise to a resolution to do something that can be done; it is quite another to bring forth the sort of determination that says, "Even if it cannot be done, I will do it!" Such a fierce resolve itself can be a strong inner condition allowing us to accomplish those aspirations that *are* possible.

Reinforcing the power of our aspirations by daring to aspire to the impossible serves us greatly when we seek to accomplish the possible. It makes our mind even vaster and our convictions even stronger than the adversity we encounter in the course of pursuing those aspirations we *can* bring to completion. Our vast aspirations make our mind so open and spacious that we do not become discouraged or give up easily. The unbounded attitude we have generated by nurturing impossible aspirations reaches so far that it is not limited by what is possible. Obstacles do routinely arise in the course of pursuing any aspiration. But none of these ordinary, limited obstacles will appear insurmountable. They will be no match for our boundless and limitless resolution.

Once we have stabilized and intensified the aspirations that can be accomplished, we will not be able to bear to sit still, only hoping and praying, but will be moved to create the causes to make it happen. Strengthening aspirations and then setting intentions is an important step, but ultimately this must lead us to the stage when aspirations manifest in action.

As we begin to enact our aspirations, it helps to keep clear the important difference between expectations and aspirations. This difference parallels the difference between desire and need. What we desire is just something we want. Our desire may have no real reason accompanying it. What we need always has more compelling reasons to accomplish it. Our need itself is a real reason to keep going. Even if we encounter more difficulties, we know we must continue until we achieve the goals. With expectations, the emphasis is on our desire for something, and there is much less focus on the steps required to fulfill that desire. We are gazing so fixedly at the result that we hardly notice the need to create the causes. With aspirations, we see the aim as something vitally important and are willing to create whatever causes are needed.

THE POWER OF IMAGINATION

In moving from aspiration to action, imagination plays an important role. Our imagination is one of the inner conditions that can allow other inner conditions to come forth and interact with outer conditions to impact the world around us. In other words, our imagination helps shape the reality we are creating. This does not mean we live in a fantasy world. On the contrary, our imagination allows us to dare to consider making our aspirations a reality. But our enacting of our aspirations cannot simply take place in our mind. At some point, it must become reality. At that point, our imagination can also offer us a blueprint for mapping our aspirations onto the world. When our aspiration has grown to full strength and our imagination actually shows us how things could be, the transition from the realm of dreams and ideas into full-blooded reality can be spontaneous and natural.

In Buddhism, and especially within Tibetan Buddhism, there is a long tradition of envisioning our inner qualities in a kind of physical form. We give names to such imagined forms and describe their features. For example, in the case of compassion, we imagine that our altruistic capacity takes the form of an enlightened being whose very essence is unconditional compassion. This taps into our creative imagination, using it to turn abstract principles into something that feels real, alive, and effective. Qualities like compassion, responsibility, or wisdom do little good to us or others if they stay stuck in our heads or locked up inside us. We need to bring them forth in a form that can be seen and felt in the world.

The point of practices that exercise our imagination in this way is to move from ideas to feelings, and finally to life. Here is an example of how such practices work. We imagine the very embodiment of compassion in the form of a being we call Chenrezig. We visualize Chenrezig seated in our heart on a disk made of moonlight. We are familiar with the moon in the sky, radiating its gentle light in all directions, so we try to imagine that our own compassion likewise radiates out from us. It yearns to go forth to all beings, just as universally as moonlight does. It shows no partiality, withholding itself from some and bathing others fully in its light. We also draw on the idea that moonlight is felt to be cooling, as if the light itself carried a cooling breeze. Evoking that idea, we try to feel that our compassion can similarly take away the heat of anger. In this way, we use our creative imagination to make our practice more dynamic.

At a certain point in the visualization, the moonlight comes to feel so bright and intense that it cannot stay within our heart. Of course, an imagined moonlight in the heart cannot ease the suffering of beings. It needs to move outside us, to a place where it becomes freely available to embrace others with its cooling light. Even as the rays of the moon illuminate effortlessly and without discrimination, so too can the radiance of an altruistic heart. This is the final aim of our visualization practice: to develop and intensify our compassion so that we act spontaneously and continuously to end the suffering around us.

ENGAGING THE SENSES

Such practices of the imagination help us to begin engaging our senses. At first, we are interacting mentally with an image of the qualities we seek to see active in the world. But we need to keep going, using the vitality and momentum that our imagination gives us, until our whole being is engaged in compassion.

I have spoken of the importance of direct sensory experience. Since an increasing percentage of our contact with others is now taking place through electronic means, we need to take special care that our connections to others do not come to seem abstract or ethereal. The Internet places our relationships in the cloud, but we need to live our relationships here on the ground. In direct contact, our warm feelings can truly warm one another and be translated into real action. This last step is key. Connectedness, compassion, and all the other values of interdependence must rise to action.

Direct, sensory contact with others helps bring compassion from inside your head and heart out into the world. Your sense perceptions themselves become compassionate, and from there your physical movements likewise become compassionate in nature. When this happens, you naturally are poised to act at every opportunity to end others' suffering. You are living compassion, not just having an intellectual engagement with it. When the compassion in your heart saturates you, as you listen to another person, your ears become ears of compassion. The eyes you see them with become eyes of compassion.

You must engage all your senses—in fact, all of your resources— to live your connections with others to their fullest potential. If the senses are left out, you are limiting the possibility that your compassionate awareness will lead to action.

SHARING ASPIRATIONS

We all have tremendous virtuous potential. But our virtue needs support, and we ourselves can give it much of the initial support it needs.

Some of our qualities, like compassion, are naturally positive. But we also have other skills and aptitudes that are neutral and could be used for either good or bad. These include such things as our technological, communication, and scientific abilities. Too often these are directed to negative aims. Many video games today visualize killing and glorify violence. Advertising promotes envy, greed, and selfishness. We could make significant change just by consciously harnessing our various skills to positive aims instead. Science and technology could have a huge impact through relatively small measures if they were guided by our most positive aspirations.

We can start by sharing our hopes and dreams. As our aspirations find expression outside the limits of our own hearts, we discover that many others harbor similar aspirations. Anchoring ourselves in shared aspirations, we need not put off acting until we can create a massive movement for change. The opportunities to start shifting things are there all around us all the time.

The fact that you are reading this book reflects a deep concern for the world and a willingness to explore other options for the direction it is moving. Many people are wishing for a better future for the world, for world peace, and for an end to the destruction of our natural environment. A huge number of individuals harbor truly beautiful and wholesome aspirations for the world. But I think maybe their aspirations feel lonely, because they have not united with others' aspirations.

At a certain point, a noble aspiration alone in our heart can slowly come to lose its virtuous power if it does not receive the support it needs. If we feel that we are just one individual isolated in our tiny corner of the planet, we may feel helpless in the face of the challenges it would take to realize such vast aspirations. But people are waiting all around the world to connect, to join others with similar thoughts and dreams. When we come together and interact to exchange views and dreams, we will find that many others share our aspirations. One of my aims here is to emphasize just how widely held the aspirations for a better world are.

As we connect with those all around us who share our aspirations, we find that we have many more friends who can join us in accompanying our shared virtues. The awareness that we are not alone naturally encourages us and becomes a supportive condition for the ultimate fulfillment of our aspirations. We can provide the noble aspirations and virtuous intentions, but they need supporting conditions to become reality. The sharing of aspirations is one such condition. Therefore, along with knowing how to nourish our own noble intentions and aspirations, it is important to know how to support others' aspirations.

Aspirations flourish when they are shared. As they flourish, our shared aspirations can mutually support and reinforce one another. We will naturally move ahead to the next phase in developing aspirations, which is the shift to action. When shared aspirations yield collective action, real change is sure to occur.

Even in periods of world history when many atrocities were committed, there was no dearth of people with good hearts and virtuous qualities. For example, it is not the case that there were no good people in Germany during World War II. There are many inspiring stories of individuals who did find the courage to act even in terrifying conditions. Surely there were many good people, but not enough of them spoke up. Many were paralyzed by their fear or fell prey to apathy. Based on that, a mass genocide could take place around them.

There is a famous quote that describes how such a thing could occur. Speaking during the Nazi era, the German pastor Martin Niemöller said something like: "First they came for the socialists and I said nothing. Then they came for the homosexuals, and I said nothing. Then they came for the Jews, and I said nothing. Finally they came for me, and there was no one left to speak up."

Although the world has many good people, the virtue inside us does not automatically translate into action. Even in situations where the possible retribution is far less severe, out of dislike of confrontation or criticism, we might lack the courage to speak out. The absence of this necessary quality prevents our compassion from manifesting outside us. This is an important reminder that our inner qualities not only interact with outer conditions; they are also interconnected mutually. In order for one positive inner quality to flourish and lead to action, it requires the presence of other positive qualities within us to serve as its supportive conditions. For compassion to blossom, we need to nourish our courage, our altruistic aspirations, our empathy, our sense of responsibility, our wisdom, and many of the other qualities we have been exploring in this book. To bring together the right outer conditions for others to flourish we must bring together the right qualities within ourselves. This is an important reason why it is so essential that we tend to our own inner world with great care.

It is true that just being a good person—having cultivated a whole garden of goodness within yourself—does not mean you are in a good position to act virtuously. There may be more good people in bad situations than in good situations. But precisely to encourage good people to be more active in manifesting their goodness—in order for their positive aspirations and noble intentions to be enacted to bring about positive change in the world—we must join together. We must share our aspirations and virtuous strength, to produce a huge positive momentum, so that good people can stand up and speak out. Our efforts to cultivate the right inner conditions within ourselves can become a condition for others to do the same.

Our actions change the world. How we act depends on the intentions and attitudes that form within us. Bringing together the right environment within us allows us to respond well to the environment around us. Inner conditions and outer conditions interact; the interplay between them creates the reality in which we live. The work that I have been describing is precisely this—working with the inner conditions of interdependence in order to transform the outer conditions and thus change the world.

OUT INTO THE WORLD

I have shared what little I have to offer from the heart with a genuine wish to be of some benefit. I did so to the best of my abilities, although this does not really make up for the fact that I am not highly learned and I do not possess a wide experience of the world. But maybe that is not so important, because the most valuable lessons you will gain about living interdependence, about how to live fully in an interconnected world, will not come from this book.

Reading about interdependence in a book or hearing about it in a lecture is no substitute for real-life experience. Your own experience can be your best teacher. You can review your past experiences and live new ones with fresh eyes. You can arrive as a first-time visitor to each new moment that opens up for you.

Go beyond watching interdependence at work around you. Live it yourself—not as a theory but as what gives value to your life. Feel it in your every breath. Enact it in your every step. Bring your most noble aspirations out into the world, share them with others, and take action.

I too join my aspirations with yours, so that together we can serve as conditions for all beings on this planet to flourish.

Dedication

I PRAY THAT YOUR LIFE will be happy—not with just a light happiness but a deep and weighty happiness. Not with just happy feelings, but with wise happiness. Do not be satisfied with temporary pleasant sensations in the name of happiness, but seek out intelligent and wise happiness.

It is possible to be happy in all circumstances, if you draw on your inner resource of wisdom—wisdom that knows what true happiness is.

Editors' Acknowledgments

THE TEACHINGS that form the basis for this book were given by His Holiness the Karmapa over the course of three weeks in his residence in Dharamsala, India, to a group of students from the University of Redlands, and were led and facilitated by the coeditors of this book. The classes formed a course for which the students received college credit toward their degrees. Without the unflagging support of the Karmapa Office of Administration for the unconventional interactions between the Karmapa and university students, this book would not have come into existence. We would particularly like to thank the administration's Deputy General Secretary Karma Chungyalpa, as well as Khenpo Tenkyong, Khenpo Lekshey, Yeshe Namgyal, Gyaltsen Sonam, Karma Tsering, and Tashi Paljor. His Holiness spoke much of the time in Tibetan, and Ngodup Tsering Burkhar kindly provided oral interpretation on the spot, for which we offer our gratitude. The text you have read in this book is based on a fresh written translation that was prepared later directly from the Tibetan and combined with His Holiness' English for the sake of consistency.

Our thanks to the administration at the University of Redlands, who embrace the opportunity of ongoing friendship with His Holiness the Karmapa as a unique and genuine form of cross-cultural, global education: President Ralph Kuncl, Provost Kathy Ogren, Director of the Johnston Center Kelly Hankin, and Karen's colleagues in Religious Studies and the Johnston Center for Integrative Studies.

Our thanks to the students in the group from the University of Redlands: Sarah Bey, Eliza Craig, Ellen Douglass, Daniel Driscoll, Elana Gurewitz, Kate Leung, James MacNee, Virginia Osterman, Sophie Schuyler, Ian Spencer, and Danica Teyssier. Thank you to Professor Daniel Kiefer, for joining the group with heartfelt commitment and pragmatic on-the-ground assistance. This group's efforts to meet the challenges of living interdependently during our time in India while receiving these teachings from His Holiness the Karmapa were an essential condition for the creation of this book. Our deep gratitude for the generosity and compassion of the nuns of the Dharmadatta Nuns' Community, who hosted the students, arranging the logistics of their stay and generally caring for their needs during their time in Dharamsala.

Our thanks to Karen's family: Ed, Ben, and Rebekah Murphy for their commitment to the connections that make this project possible; their understanding that Karen's focus would be dedicated elsewhere is yet another example of the ways that the inner resources of interdependence support the external conditions for contributing to friends known and unknown.

A final debt of gratitude goes to all those who supported the Dharmadatta Nuns' Community, making it possible for Damchö to devote her time to working on this book and for the nuns of the community to host the student group during its time in Dharamsala.

May all those who were conditions for this book to come into being partake of its merits.

About the Author

AS THE SPIRITUAL HEAD of the 900-year-old Karma Kagyu lineage of Tibetan Buddhism, His Holiness the Seventeenth Karmapa, Ogyen Trinley Dorje, has emerged as an important thought leader for our time. Since his dramatic escape from Tibet to India in 2000, the Karmapa has played a key role in preserving Tibetan religion and culture. He has been described as "a world spiritual leader for the twenty-first century" and has inspired millions of people worldwide to take action on social and environmental issues. At the age of thirty-one, the Karmapa's message has particularly resonated with young people, whom he encourages to take responsibility to create a more compassionate future for the planet.

"Karmapa" literally means "He Who Performs the Activities of the Buddha" and the Karmapa lineage itself is known for putting Buddhist principles into action. The Khoryug association that he founded has transformed over fifty-five monasteries across the Himalayan region into local centers for environmental activism. Leading on women's issues, in January 2015 the Karmapa made the historic announcement that he will establish full ordination for women, a long-awaited step within Tibetan Buddhism.

REACHING OUT TO YOUTH

The Karmapa frequently seeks out opportunities for sustained inter-actions with university students and young professionals. He engages annually with groups of students at a number of Indian universities and with Tibetan student groups; he has also held several series of meetings with students from Europe and North America. The prece-dent was set for these interactions in 2011, by the first series of classes with students from the University of Redlands, also organized by the coeditors. Those meetings resulted in his earlier book, *The Heart Is Noble: Changing the World from the Inside Out*, in which the Kar-mapa speaks to his generation on the major challenges facing society today, including gender issues, food justice, rampant consumerism, and the environmental crisis.

A leader of the new century, His Holiness the Karmapa makes effective use of technology to transmit and teach the Dharma widely. When he delivered a talk at a TED conference in Bangalore in 2009, he was the youngest speaker to have done so at that time. His teach-ings are usually transmitted online via live webcast with simultane-ous translation into as many as fourteen languages.

MUSICIAN, ARTIST, AND POET

His Holiness the Karmapa engages in a wide range of artistic activ-ities. He paints, draws calligraphy, writes poetry and plays, and composes music. Preserving and renewing Tibetan artistic forms, the Karmapa has written and produced several plays that combine ele-ments of traditional Tibetan opera and modern theater. His first play, a drama on the life of the great Tibetan yogi Milarepa, was attended by twenty thousand people at a single live performance in India, and is being published in an English translation.

The Seventeenth Karmapa, Ogyen Trinley Dorje, was born in 1985 to a family of nomads in the remote highlands of the Tibetan plateau and spent the first years of his life in a pristine environment free of modern conveniences, electricity, and motor vehicles.

When he was recognized as the reincarnation of the Sixteenth Karmapa at the age of seven, he left this nomadic lifestyle behind. He was formally enthroned as the Seventeenth Karmapa with two of the three living heads of his lineage officiating. Once installed in his monastic seat of Tsurphu Monastery in central Tibet, at the age of eight he delivered his first public religious discourse to an audience of over twenty thousand people.

ESCAPE TO RELIGIOUS FREEDOM IN INDIA

In the years to come, the Karmapa would face numerous challenges in his efforts to perform his spiritual activities. Concerned that he would be unable to meet his religious obligations, he decided to escape from Tibet at the age of fourteen, seeking the freedom to fulfill his religious responsibilities. He has been living in Dharamsala in northern India, a short distance from the residence of His Holiness the Dalai Lama, with whom he continues to enjoy a close relationship of mentor and protégé to this day.

The Karmapa receives thousands of visitors at his residence in northern India and discusses practical global solutions with people from all around the world. In 2004 His Holiness assumed responsibility for the Kagyu Monlam, an annual gathering to make aspiration prayers for world peace, which is held in Bodhgaya, the site where the Buddha became enlightened. Under his guidance, this annual event has grown to over twelve thousand participants.

In 2009 the Karmapa founded Khoryug (Tibetan for "environment") and chairs this association of over fifty-five Buddhist monasteries and nunneries across the Himalayan region. His efforts have educated thousands of monks and nuns, mobilizing them to lead their local communities on environmental issues and to implement projects that have turned their own homes into eco-monasteries.

In 2015 the Seventeenth Karmapa made history with his announcement that he would take the first step in establishing bhikshuni ordination for nuns within Tibetan Buddhism. In 2014 the Karmapa had already instituted an annual Arya Kshema Winter Dharma Gathering for Karma Kagyu nuns, extended access to rigorous education for nuns, and arranged for empowerment initiatives in the nunneries. Within his own school of Tibetan Buddhism, he has been modernizing religious practices yet remains firmly rooted in tradition as he reinvigorates monastic discipline in his lineage.

The Seventeenth Karmapa has been granted an honorary doctoral degree by the institution whose students formed the audience for the teachings contained in this book. The University of Redlands awarded him this degree in recognition of his work in educating youth to assume social responsibility and act for meaningful change. The Karmapa has also been awarded Yale University's prestigious Chubb Fellowship for his global leadership on environmental issues.

What to Read Next from Wisdom Publications

MINDFULNESS IN PLAIN ENGLISH
Bhante Gunaratana

"A classic—one of the very best English sources for authoritative explanations of mindfulness."—Daniel Goleman, author of *Emotional Intelligence*

THE MIDDLE WAY
Faith Grounded in Reason
His Holiness the Dalai Lama
Translated by Thupten Jinpa

"How fortunate we are to have access to these brilliant teachings given by the Dalai Lama. A truly inspiring book."—*Mandala*

THE BUDDHA'S TEACHINGS ON SOCIAL AND COMMUNAL HARMONY
An Anthology of Discourses from the Pāli Canon
Bhikkhu Bodhi

"A fantastic inspiration for all of us who value and wish to foster a more harmonious world."—Sharon Salzberg, author of *Lovingkindness*

About Wisdom Publications

Wisdom Publications is the leading publisher of classic and contemporary Buddhist books and practical works on mindfulness. To learn more about us or to explore our other books, please visit our website at wisdompubs.org or contact us at the address below.

Wisdom Publications
199 Elm Street
Somerville, MA 02144 USA

We are a 501(c)(3) organization, and donations in support of our mission are tax deductible.

Wisdom Publications is affiliated with the Foundation for the Preservation of the Mahayana Tradition (FPMT).